Historic Aberdeen

the archaeological implications of development

E Patricia **Dennison**

Judith **Stones**

D1613077

the Scottish burgh survey

HISTORIC SCOTLAND

in association with

SCOTTISH CULTURAL PRESS

ABERDEEN
CITY COUNCIL

ARTS & RECREATION DEPARTMENT

publication   Historic Scotland *in association with* Scottish Cultural Press
First published 1997

copyright   © Historic Scotland 1997
The moral right of the authors has been asserted.

editorial   Olwyn Owen

design   Christina Unwin

printing   George Morrison at BPC-AUP Aberdeen Ltd

ISSN   1358 0272

Scottish Cultural Press ISBN   1 898218 39 0

**all distribution
and sales enquiries**
Scottish burgh survey   Scottish Cultural Press
Unit 14 . Leith Walk Business Centre
130 Leith Walk
Edinburgh
EH6 5DT
telephone *0131* 555 5950 . facsimile *0131* 555 5018

all other enquiries
Aberdeen   ■ Aberdeen City Council
City Arts and Recreation Department
Art Gallery
Schoolhill
Aberdeen
AB10 1FQ
telephone *01224* 646333 . facsimile *01224* 213546

■ Historic Scotland
Longmore House
Salisbury Place
Edinburgh
EH9 1SH
telephone *0131* 668 8600 . facsimile *0131* 668 8699

**British Library cataloguing
in publication data**   A catalogue record for this book is available from the British Library

contents

OLD ABERDEEN

acknowledgements   A number of individuals and institutions have given valuable assistance and support   vii
during the preparation of this volume. The authors wish to express particular gratitude to
the following:

Dr Harold Booton.

Ms Alison Cameron, Dr Michael Dey, Dr Anne Johnston and Mr Charles Murray, **Aberdeen City Council, Arts and Recreation Department**.

Miss Judith Cripps, **Aberdeen City Council Archives**.

Dr Grant Simpson and Mrs Anne Turner Simpson.

Mrs Hilary Flenley.

Dr Iain Fraser.

Professor Michael Lynch, **Department of Scottish History, University of Edinburgh**.

Dr Leslie J Macfarlane.

Mr Colin A McLaren, **Aberdeen University Archives**.

Mr Aidan Mulkerrin.

Mrs Melissa Seddon, **Historic Scotland**.

Dr John Smith, **Department of Geography, University of Aberdeen**.

Mr Geoffrey Stell, **Royal Commission on the Ancient and Historical Monuments of Scotland**.

Mrs Sylvia Stevenson.

figures 6, **7**, **18**, **19**, **25**, **30**, **32**, **35**, **41**, **46** & **47** are reproduced by permission of **Aberdeen City Libraries**.

figures 1, **2**, **3**, **8**, **9**, **10**, **12**, **13**, **17**, **22**, **23**, **24**, **27**, **29**, **31**, **34**, **37**, **38**, **39**, **42**, **43**, **44**, **45**, **48**, **49**, **50** & **51** are based upon the Ordnance Survey 1:50, 000 and 1:1250 map series, with permission of **The Controller of Her Majesty's Stationery Office**. © Crown Copyright.

figures 15, **16** & **36** are reproduced by permission of **Historic Scotland**. © Crown Copyright, Historic Scotland.

foreword   The history of Aberdeen is a tale of two burghs, Old Aberdeen and New Aberdeen, which began life as two geographically close but separate entities, and developed in very different ways. Old Aberdeen's influences were ecclesiastical and academic; it was established as a bishopric in 1125/1130, becoming a burgh of barony in 1489, and its prestige was further enhanced with the founding of King's College by Bishop Elphinstone in 1495. New Aberdeen, on the other hand, developed due to its importance as a market and trading centre, having been granted the status of a king's burgh in the twelfth century. Both burghs were adversely affected by the Reformation, and while New Aberdeen's trade and new industries enabled it to develop and expand over the following centuries, Old Aberdeen was unable to compete and remained a modestly-sized town. Old and New Aberdeen joined to form the city of Aberdeen in 1891. *Historic Aberdeen* investigates the parallel history and development of the two burghs, showing how this was affected both by local factors—such as topography—and by national events. The influences of trade, religion and education on the burghs' physical evolution are also examined. Building on this information, *Historic Aberdeen* explores what archaeological evidence of the burghs' historic past might survive beneath the streets, buildings and open spaces of present-day Aberdeen.

This account of the history and archaeology of Old Aberdeen and New Aberdeen is one of a series of reports on the historic burghs of Scotland—known collectively as the *Scottish burgh survey*—all of which have been commissioned by **Historic Scotland** and its predecessors. Some fifty-six burghs have been surveyed during previous campaigns of the Scottish Burgh Survey (1978–90). The present campaign of burgh survey began in 1994 and, for the first time, includes formal publication. *Historic Aberdeen* is the sixth volume to be published in the new series.

Historic Aberdeen was prepared for Historic Scotland within the **Archaeological Unit, City Arts and Recreation Division, Aberdeen District Council**, under the direction of its Keeper of Archaeology, Judith Stones, one of the main authors of this book. The other main author is historian Dr E Patricia Dennison, Director of the **Centre for Scottish Urban History, Department of Scottish History, University of Edinburgh**. Dr John Smith of the **Department of Geography, University of Aberdeen**, has kindly contributed a chapter on the physical setting of the burgh. All the maps and other line drawings were prepared within the Aberdeen District Council Archaeological Unit by Clare Yarrington and Jan Dunbar. Photographs (other than historic) were the work of Roger Brown, Eleanor Hutcheon, the late Lynn Duncan, and Richard White. The project was managed for Historic Scotland by Olwyn Owen, Inspector of Ancient Monuments, who is also general editor of the series.

This survey of historic Aberdeen was entirely funded by Historic Scotland. Historic Scotland acknowledges with gratitude the generous support provided towards the costs of printing this book by **Aberdeen District Council**. Further copies of the book may be obtained from **Scottish Cultural Press**, Unit 14, Leith Walk Business Centre, 130 Leith Walk, Edinburgh EH6 5DT.

Historic Scotland
February 1997

the Scottish burgh survey

A

1   Use the colour-coded maps on p 30 **figure 8** and p 96 **figure 42** (New and Old
     Aberdeen respectively) and/or the **general index** to locate a particular site (normally
     the site of a development proposal).

2   **Green areas** are designated as archaeologically sensitive. If the site is in a green area,
     it is possible that any proposal involving ground disturbance may encounter
     archaeological remains. Seek appropriate archaeological advice as early as possible.

3   **Red areas** are Scheduled Ancient Monuments or properties in the care of the
     Secretary of State for Scotland, and are protected by law. Consult Historic
     Scotland.

4   Use the maps on pp 32 **figure 9**, 83 **figure 37** and 98 **figure 43** (New Aberdeen,
     harbour area and Old Aberdeen respectively) to determine into which area of the
     burgh the site falls (one of Areas 1–20), and turn to the relevant area in the **area by
     area assessment** for a fuller account.

5   Use the **general index** (pp 109–21) for rapid access to information specific to a site,
     street or named feature of the town.

step 1

As a working manual, the first point of reference is the colour-coded maps on p 30 **figure 8**
and p 96 **figure 42** (New and Old Aberdeen respectively).

The **red areas** are **protected by law**. Under the provisions of the Ancient Monuments
and Archaeological Areas Act 1979 all development proposals which affect them require
the prior written consent of the Secretary of State (Scheduled Monument Consent) in
addition to any planning permission required. These provisions are administered on behalf
of the Secretary of State by Historic Scotland. **All applications for planning permission
which affect either the site or setting of a Scheduled Ancient Monument (red area) must be
referred to Historic Scotland,** acting for the Secretary of State in terms of Section 15(j)(v) of
the Town and Country Planning (General Development Procedure) (Scotland) Order 1992
and Section 5(e) of its Amendment (No. 2) Order 1994. *All enquiries regarding prospective
development proposals in or adjacent to red areas should be referred to Historic Scotland for advice as early
as possible.*

The **green areas** are **potentially archaeologically sensitive** and may retain significant
sub-surface archaeological information. *Consultation should take place with the Keeper of
Archaeology, City Arts and Recreation Department, where any development proposal or enquiry involving
ground disturbance is being considered,* including car parks, road schemes, environmental
improvements, landscaping and drainage schemes, as well as the usual range of
development and re-development proposals in built-up areas. There is no necessity for a
consultation where ground disturbance is not in prospect, such as applications for change
of use of a building. There may, however, be a requirement to obtain *planning permission* or,
in the case of a listed building, *listed building consent* or, if demolition works are proposed
within a conservation area, *conservation area consent.* In such instances, early consultation
with the staff of the local authority planning department will always be helpful.

If in doubt whether consultation is necessary, please refer to the Keeper of Archaeology,
City Arts and Recreation Department, and the Council's Planning and Strategic
Development Department. *It should always be borne in mind that historic standing buildings may
also contain archaeological remains, both beneath their floors and concealed within their structures.* Some
of these buildings may be listed and consequently subject to listed building control. Where
listed buildings contain, or may contain, architecturally or archaeologically significant
building fabric, the planning authority is obliged to make efforts to ensure that this is

preserved and not adversely affected by proposed building works. The Planning Department holds full lists of the listed buildings in Old and New Aberdeen (all categories).

step 2

In this new series of burgh surveys, each survey has been organised locationally, in order to assist speedy consultation on any proposed location or development site. In the case of New Aberdeen, the historic core of the town has been divided into fourteen arbitrary areas, Areas 1–14 (including the harbour area), which are shown on the plans on p30 **figure 8**, 32 **figure 9** and p 83 **figure 37**. Old Aberdeen is divided into a further six areas, Areas 15–20, shown on the plans on p 96 **figure 42** and 98 **figure 43**. The second step for the user is to consult these plans to determine into which area a specific enquiry falls.

step 3

Each area is assessed individually in the **area by area assessments** (pp 33–91 and 99–118), the commentary for each area prefaced with a detailed plan of that area. Each area assessment contains summaries of all the historical information (from documentary and cartographic sources) about known sites and monuments; basic historical and architectural information about the historic standing buildings; and the evidence from any previous archaeological work (excavations, observations and chance finds). An assessment is made of the archaeological potential of that area and, where appropriate, of specific buildings.

background chapters

Consideration of the **physical setting** of the burgh and the nature of its underlying topography is crucial to any understanding of the origins and growth of New and Old Aberdeen. An introductory chapter, kindly provided by Dr John Smith, describes Aberdeen's geography and geology, and their impact on the morphology of the town.

Unusually, this burgh survey is really a tale of two burghs: New and Old Aberdeen. The two burghs are here dealt with consecutively (in that order), and each is prefaced by a discussion of the relevant **historical background**, followed by an overview of the **archaeology** of the burgh and its remaining archaeological potential.

gazetteer

A number of important medieval and later sites and monuments lie outwith the historic cores of New and Old Aberdeen but within the modern city boundary. A selection of these sites is listed in the **gazetteer** and their significance is briefly considered. They include not only medieval sites, but also eighteenth- to early nineteenth-century industries and industrial monuments, which are of such importance for the early modern history of Aberdeen as a whole. These monuments will also require an appropriate archaeological response in the case of any proposed ground disturbance. Some of them may also be listed buildings.

It should be noted that this burgh survey only examines in detail the *medieval archaeology* of Aberdeen and Old Aberdeen. Within the city boundaries there are in addition many archaeologically sensitive areas of all periods which must be protected through the development process. For further details, the Keeper of Archaeology, City Arts and Recreation Department, should be contacted.

Any report of this nature cannot be definitive. During its preparation, a series of archaeological and historical objectives for future fieldwork and research have been identified (*see* p 119). They will be of particular interest to urban historians and archaeologists, and to those responsible for management of the archaeological resource in historic Aberdeen.

referencing

The report contains a comprehensive **general index** (including street and place names) for easy reference. A **glossary** of technical terms and a **bibliography** of all sources (primary, secondary and cartographic) have also been included.

The data accumulated during preparation of this survey, and draft copies of the completed work, are housed in the **National Monuments Record**, John Sinclair House, 16 Bernard Terrace, Edinburgh EH8 9NX, telephone *0131* 662 1456, facsimile *0131* 662 1477/1499. Full information on excavations and watching briefs is held by the Keeper of Archaeology, City Arts and Recreation Department, Art Gallery, Schoolhill, Aberdeen AB10 1FQ, telephone *01224* 646333 *extension* 250, facsimile *01224* 213546.

full reference to this report   Dennison, E P and Stones, J 1996 *Historic Aberdeen: the archaeological implications of development*, published by Historic Scotland in association with Scottish Cultural Press, Edinburgh (Scottish Burgh Survey 1997).

4

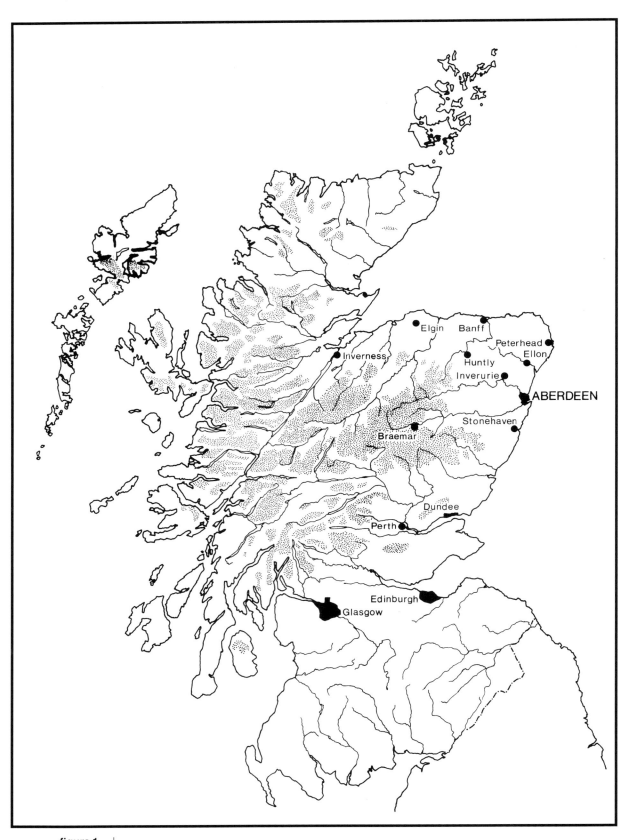

figure 1
Location of
Aberdeen
© Crown Copyright

**Aberdeen:
the physical
setting**

figures **1**, **2**, **3** *&* **4**

Dr John Smith

The historic burghs of Old and New Aberdeen lie between the twin estuaries of the Rivers Dee and Don **figures 1** *&* **3**, at a point where the character of the North Sea coast changes dramatically. To the north there are dune-fringed beaches hinged on a small number of rocky headlands; to the south, the natural rock groyne of Girdleness begins a rock-girt cliffy coastline, fringed by rocky shore platforms, and indented only by small bays and geos. Embayments of the scale of the Dee and Don estuaries are repeated on the Scottish east coast only at Montrose and the Ythan. These major embayments must have facilitated inland penetration by early historic peoples—and this is attested archaeologically to varying degrees in the Dee and Ythan valleys. Within the boundaries of medieval Aberdeen itself, flint scatters of early hunter-gatherers have been discovered capping the primary land surface, and overlain by medieval occupation horizons. At a rather later stage, such estuaries promoted the early development of sea-borne trade. Although the Dee–Don estuary is not unique on the east coast of Scotland, the combination of site characteristics encountered is unusual.

Early historical and medieval Aberdeen developed on a series of fluvioglacial sand and gravel mounds, which entirely masked the underlying Old Red Sandstones conglomerates. The southern boundary of these sandstones, which occur at the surface only on the banks of the Don between the Brig o' Balgownie and the Bridge of Don, is marked by a faultline mapped as running along the northern axis of the Dee valley, south of which outcrop Dalradian metasedimentaries.

The rising ground west of middle Union Street is underlain by granites. A series of shallow valleys, all originally carrying small streams, dissects the higher ground on the west, with most of the stream outflows originally ending in the Dee estuary or the lower Dee channel. In a sense, the solid geology is much less significant than the drift geology in determining site characteristics, and attention is therefore here concentrated on the latter— that is, the distribution of the superficial deposits, their topographic form, and the many intervening depressions, which were originally marshy or water-filled.

The series of sand and gravel mounds aligned roughly north–south runs between the Dee and the Don—linking the medieval nuclei of Old Aberdeen and New Aberdeen via the Spital. Outliers occur in the form of the Broad Hill and Woolmanhill, and also in the Ferryhill area where the Old Statistical Account records 'many curious little sandhills, lying in all different directions and moulded into various forms, seemingly by the retiring of some immense quantity of water'.[1]

Douglas, describing the Ferryhill environment in 1782, notes 'little conical hills which were generally overrun with heath and furze, while the flat bottoms between them were drenched with stagnant water'.[2] As the regional slope between the Dee and Don valleys runs generally eastwards, these mounds, constructed by meltwater activities during the waning of the last icesheet, tended to impede the natural drainage, leading to the formation of small lochs and ill-drained areas. The mounds overlooking the estuary of the Dee formed the medieval nucleus of Aberdeen. The town's situation on a series of small 'hills' struck most early travellers and writers—for example in 1685, Baillie Alexander Skene wrote that 'Aberdeen is pleasantly situated upon three hills which are all joined together by easy descents so that in the middle of the streets, they [the hills] are scarcely discernible' **figure 5**.[3] And in 1661 James Gordon, parson and cartographer, wrote that 'in our age, the most considerable part of the 'city' standeth on three hills—the Castell Hill, St Katherine's Hill and the Gallowgate Hill. The city itself is situated betwixt these three—or at least the best part of it—the swelling of these hills is hardly discerned by such as walk along the streets, yet their height is apparent to those who dwell in the suburbs or without the town'.[4]

While many commentators concentrate on these three key 'hills', the particularly detailed map **figure 6** and description of James Gordon names a dozen hills in total—Ferryhill, Woolmanhill, Castle Hill, Broad Hill, Heading Hill, Gallowhill, Gallowgate Hill (also termed Wyndmill Hill), St Katherine's Hill, Spital Hill, Tillydrone Hill, Kettle Hills and Clayhills.

To the east of the key nuclei, the natural sand dune ridges and sand links acted as further obstacles to easterly stream flow, leading to the diversion of streams for short distances subparallel to the North Sea coast, as seen in the lower section of the Powis Burn (Tile Burn). Inland of the sand and gravel mounds lay a higher and less attractive section of country whose characteristics were noted both by James Gordon and by Anderson in his *Agriculture of Aberdeenshire*. The latter notes that 'the city is surrounded on all sides by a zone of the most barren ground that can anywhere be seen, about six to eight miles in breadth'.[5] The former describes fields immediately outside the town 'gates' as fruitful of corn, but adds that within a mile lay a barren landscape of marshes and moors.[6] The *Old Statistical Account* describes the same high ground as 'not many years ago covered with stones and heath'.[7] The massive consumption dykes characteristic of the zone beyond the line of the Inner Marches are an impressive reminder of the stoniness of the soils in the higher parts. Many such areas were to be trenched and cleared of stones in the late eighteenth century (motivated by the sale of stones for the London market), and thus brought into agriculture. These heavy stony glacial till deposits are thus capped in the medieval kernel of the town by the fluvioglacial sands and gravels, creating springs, seepages and groundwater supplies, which together with the naturally-impounded lochs, provided potential water supplies for the infant burgh, perched on the dry ridges.

Lochans and burns were vital natural resources in early times, driving the town's cornmills and providing sources of industrial and domestic water supplies, while the stream and loch banks were extensively used as bleachfields. The two largest bodies of standing water lay immediately landward of the Gallowgate–Spital ridge, and its northerly continuation on the axis of the High Street. The Loch of New Aberdeen **figure 5** probably had a maximum extent of one hundred acres and was fed principally by the Spital Burn and the West Burn. By the time of James Gordon's map of 1661 **figure 6**, it is significantly termed 'The marsh called the Loch'. The remaining areas of open water were described as 'filthily defiled and corrupted' and, apart from sediment infill, much of its natural input of water had been abstracted, possibly as early as the twelfth century to supply water to the Broadgate area. The other historic loch occupied the hollow now mainly utilised as the playing fields of St Machar Academy. It provided a water supply for the separate settlement of Old Aberdeen. Increasing pollution and water abstraction in the core areas of the town pushed the search for quality water westwards, even while New Aberdeen remained physically constricted to the east of the lower Denburn valley.

Around the shores of the Dee and Don estuaries, raised estuarine deposits provided 'a stratum of excellent clay'. This formed the basis of the Seaton and Clayhills tileworks and, presumably, of the local medieval pottery industry (*see* p 123). The estuaries themselves, in contrast to these largely relict landforms and deposits, were geomorphologically active environments. Their constantly changing network of channels, gravel inches and entrance sandpits provided problems of flooding and siltation which tested the skill of the early mariners. The earliest known location of shoreworks at the foot of the Shiprow confirmed the importance of the scouring activities of the Denburn in allowing the smallest of vessels access at high tide to within a few hundred metres of the medieval core of the burgh. As with the expansion from the medieval town, so in the Dee estuary, major engineering improvements were achieved only towards the end of the eighteenth century. To all intents and purposes, therefore, the situation of New Aberdeen portrayed in James Gordon's map of 1661 **figure 6** probably represents the pattern as it existed from the twelfth century onwards.

Despite the difficult and extremely varied nature of this terrain, Aberdeen was, in a sense, a likely site for an early burgh because it lay on the edge of an environmentally favoured lowland plain and hard by an estuary mouth with the potential for sea-borne trade—despite the physical problems of flooding and siltation. Its potential is best assessed by comparing it to the limited regional array of east coast locations with these basic characteristics. In medieval Scotland, any cluster of population with such comparable advantages was destined to function and further develop as a collecting, distribution and small-scale manufacturing centre.

Immediately beyond the nucleus lay the arable and grazing ground of the burgh, the Croftlands, the outer boundary of which formed the line of the Town's Inner Marches.

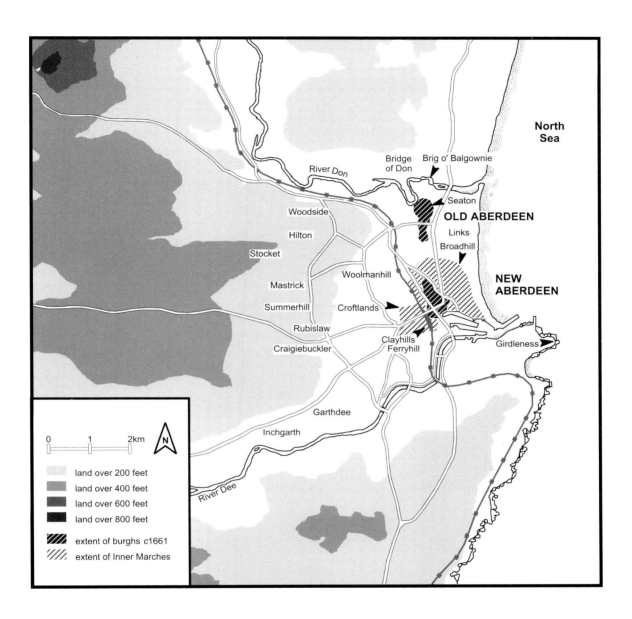

North
Sea

OLD ABERDEEN

NEW
ABERDEEN

Girdleness

Bridge of Don · Brig o' Balgownie · Seaton · Links · Broadhill · Woodside · Hilton · Stocket · Woolmanhill · Mastrick · Croftlands · Summerhill · Rubislaw · Clayhills · Ferryhill · Craigiebuckler · Garthdee · Inchgarth · River Don · River Dee

0 1 2km N

land over 200 feet
land over 400 feet
land over 600 feet
land over 800 feet
extent of burghs c1661
extent of Inner Marches

figure 2
The physical setting
of Aberdeen
© Crown Copyright

This runs approximately along the inner edge of the Links and the Broad Hill to the Spital, thence southwards towards Causewayend and Gilcomston, and then south towards Justice Mills (Holburn Junction), and finally southwestwards towards the original margin of the Dee estuary to meet it on roughly the site of the Clayhills Rail Depot. Beyond, stretching out to the line of the Outer March, lay the Common Lands—chiefly the 'barren ring' of stony soils described by Gordon and Anderson, including the Stocket Forest bestowed by Bruce's 1319 charter, together with other estates added to the burgh's resources by purchase—Rubislaw in 1379, Woodside in 1459, Hilton in 1595 and Gilcomston in 1673 (*see* pp 20, 26). Of these four, Rubislaw and Woodside, together with Stocket, formed the City Freedom Lands. From the days of the charter, apart from the timber and sporting rights, the burgh had absolute rights of possession. The croftlands included areas of some agricultural potential, especially on the flanks of the Spital where

8

the soils included wind-blown sand from the Links, while all the croftlands no doubt benefited from frequent additions of manure from the town stables. Indeed, the major developments across the Denburn in the early nineteenth century swallowed up an inner ring of nursery gardens. Beyond the original croftlands, placenames like Garthdee, Inchgarth, Summerhill, Mastrick (place of the butter churns), Craigiebuckler (place of cattle) and Balnagarth recollect the pastoral activities of the Freedom Lands while, within them, names like Sandylands, Lochfield croft and Calsay croft carry a suggestion of the original nature of the physical environment prior to its upgrading into agriculture.

Although the increase in height of buildings through the medieval period progressively reduced the visual impact of the town landforms (as noted by Skene and Gordon), eventually in the late eighteenth and early nineteenth century, improved engineering technology was to flatten, bridge and embank the 'hills'. The original site characteristics, however, remain in placenames, in the alignment of the older medieval streets, and in the distribution of known medieval archaeological sites. For a period of several hundred years, the same site as shown on Gordon's map of 1661 was successively re-used and redeveloped, progressively eating into the large areas of productive open space he shows, and, of course, benefiting from the substantial areas of prime urban land released by the events of the Reformation. Despite the relative hostility of the original site of juxtaposed mounds and hollows, these very characteristics provided the positive advantages of defence, dry site, estuary and water supplies. Major expansionist decisions, however, awaited major advances in engineering technology, spurred on by population increases and commercial development.

notes

1   *Old Statistical Account*, 19, 146.
2   Douglas, 144.
3   Skene, 212.
4   *Aberdeen Description*, 9.
5   Anderson, 18.
6   *Aberdeen Description*, 3.
7   *Old Statistical Account*, 19, 149.

New Aberdeen

A

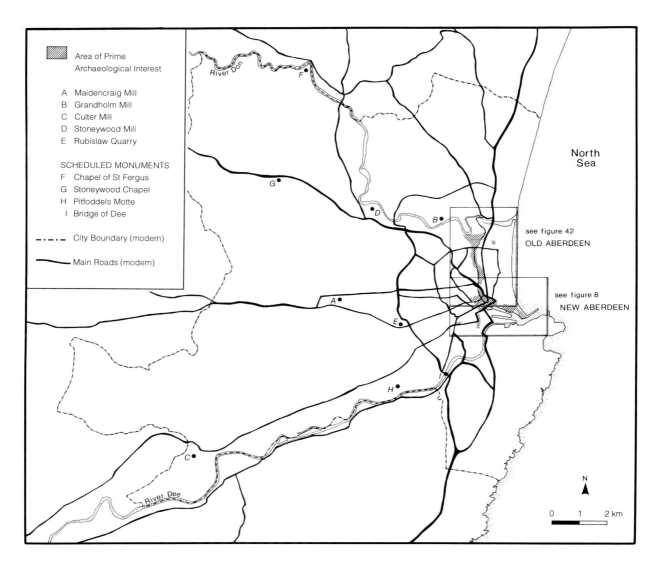

Area of Prime
Archaeological Interest

A   Maidencraig Mill
B   Grandholm Mill
C   Culter Mill
D   Stoneywood Mill
E   Rubislaw Quarry

SCHEDULED MONUMENTS
F   Chapel of St Fergus
G   Stoneywood Chapel
H   Pitfoddels Motte
I   Bridge of Dee

—·—·—   City Boundary (modern)

————   Main Roads (modern)

North
Sea

River Don

see figure 42
OLD ABERDEEN

see figure 8
NEW ABERDEEN

River Dee

N

0   1   2 km

figure 3
New and Old
Aberdeen
© Crown Copyright

**archaeological
and historical
background**

figures 4, 5 & 6

The site of present-day Aberdeen has been used by people since as early as *c* 6,000 BC. Excavations at various sites in the Green (*see* **area 10**)[1] have produced evidence of flint-knapping on the banks of the River Dee in the Mesolithic period (*c* 6,500 to 4,000 BC; literally, the Middle Stone Age). Finds of Bronze Age flint arrowheads might imply that this area was inhabited *c* 1,700 to 1,500 BC, but the exact nature of this Bronze Age human activity is uncertain.[2] By around the time of Christ, there was a settlement known to the Romans as *Devana*, which may have been on the site of Aberdeen.[3] A good case can certainly be made for accepting as Aberdeen the *Apardion* mentioned in the *Heimskringla Saga*—this medieval township was attacked by the Norwegian King Eystein in or about AD 1153.[4] Archaeological excavations in Upperkirkgate and Broad Street (*see* **area 3 & 8** respectively) have confirmed the existence of settlement in Aberdeen by the mid to late twelfth century.[5]

Documentary evidence, however, indicates that the medieval township was well established by this time. King David I (1124–53) issued at least one charter from Aberdeen;[6] Malcolm IV (1153–65) is known to have entertained the piratical Norseman, Sweyn Asleifson, in the town;[7] and William the Lion from 1174, after losing control of Roxburgh, Berwick and Edinburgh, held his larger courts at Aberdeen, as well as at Stirling and Perth.[8] By the twelfth century, Aberdeen was clearly a town of sufficient stature to house not only the king and his household, but also the magnates and prelates who attended the royal court.

the medieval burgh

defences and town ports

There is no evidence that New Aberdeen was a walled burgh in the sense that it was surrounded by a highly defensible encircling structure. Documentary and archaeological evidence suggest that the town had no defensive ditching, although the sea, the loch and other areas of surrounding marshy land offered some form of natural defence. There were proposals to ditch around the town in 1480, and to build a wall in 1529, but whether these measures were ever effected is unclear.[9] Gordon's map of 1661 **figure 6** indicates what may have been a bank along the line of Upperkirkgate Port, Netherkirkgate Port (*see* **area 7**) and the Loch, which may have been a man-made defence along the edge of the town not protected by natural features.[10] However, at the one location where this possibility was tested, 45–57 Upperkirkgate (Area 3), no relevant archaeological evidence was found.

A measure of protection to the medieval town was afforded by contiguous barricading at the tail-ends of tofts, the heid-dykes. Archaeological evidence implies that such fencing was not substantial in the early Middle Ages,[11] but these barricades did serve as a psychological barrier to entrance and exit during hours of curfew.

Many of the back walls of tofts had small gates or yetts giving access to the surrounding burghal common land and countryside and, by 1660, it was claimed that 'every garding hes its posterne'.[12] Each burgess with a back yett was held responsible for its security. In 1442, for example, it was enacted that 'al man that has back yettes close thaim, swa that thair cum na skath throw thaim to the toune under the payne of acht schillinges'.[13] This system of exclusion and isolation was reinforced by gates or ports sited at the major thoroughfares entering the town.

Documentary evidence from the first half of the fifteenth century shows that the town ports were in existence by that time. For example, it was enacted by the town council in February 1435 that 'na man na woman pas out of the portis to by anything quhil it be brocht on the market.'[14] And in 1440 five merks were demanded in payment for burgess and guild admission *ad edificationem porte in fine orientali vici castri*,[15] though this reference to 'building' a port in Castlegate might equally be interpreted as 'rebuilding'.

By the end of the Middle Ages, six ports had been constructed. Whether or not important elements of the urban scene such as the Green and the parish church stood

12

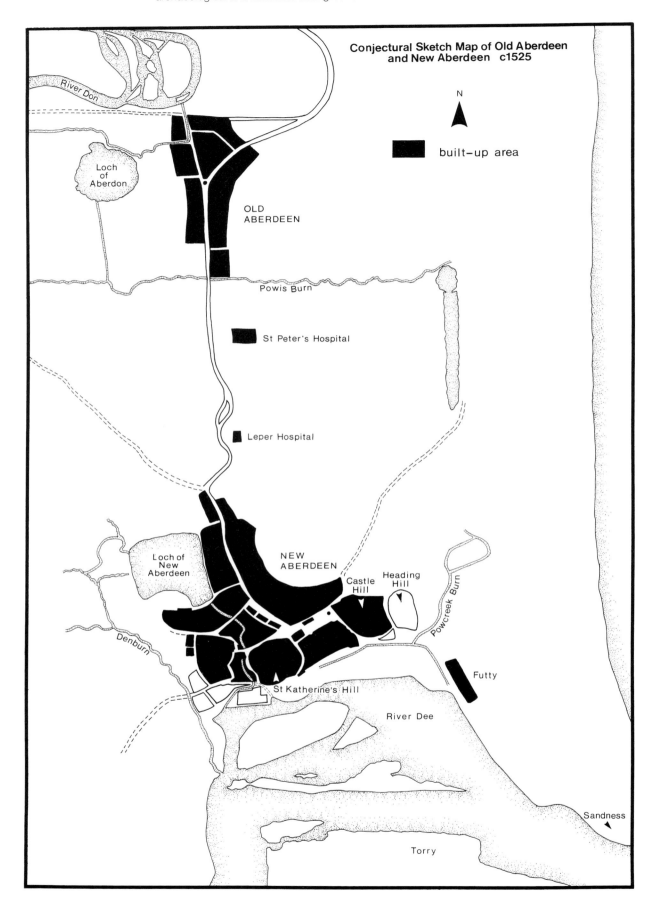

Conjectural Sketch Map of Old Aberdeen
and New Aberdeen c1525

N

■ built-up area

River Don

Loch
of
Aberdon

OLD
ABERDEEN

Powis Burn

St Peter's Hospital

Leper Hospital

Loch of
New
Aberdeen

NEW
ABERDEEN

Castle
Hill

Heading
Hill

Powcreek Burn

Denburn

St Katherine's Hill

Futty

River Dee

Sandness

Torry

figure 4
A conjectural sketch
map of New and Old
Aberdeen *c* 1525

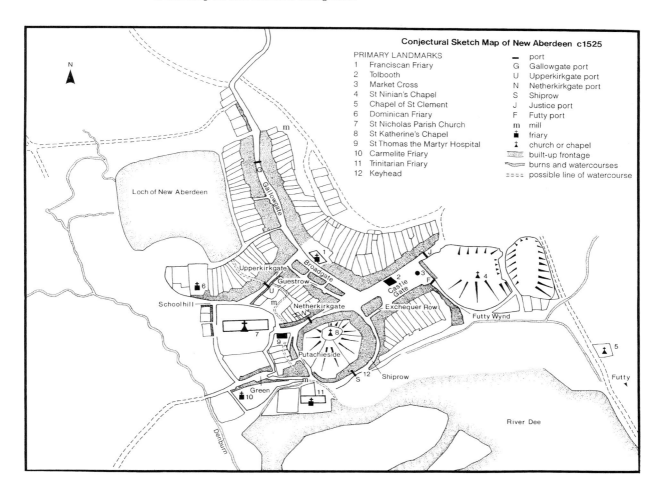

figure 5

A conjectural sketch
map of New Aberdeen
c 1525

outside these town ports is discussed below (pp 14–15). Approach from the south-west, by
Hardgate and the Green, into the town was monitored by two ports: that on Shiprow (*see*
area 11), sometimes called the Trinity Port because of its proximity to the Trinitarian
Friary, checked entry from the south side of St Katherine's Hill and from the town's
harbour; and another on Netherkirkgate (Area 7) controlled movement round the north
side of St Katherine's Hill via Putachieside from the Green. These two ports, along with
Futty Port at the south-east of Castlegate on Futty Wynd (Area 9), were to be closed to
outsiders throughout the duration of the plague in 1514, though those to the north were
to remain open (an indication of the direction from which plague was thought to be
advancing by land and sea).[16]

Futty Port's control of entrance to the Castlegate was reinforced by a further gate at
the north-eastern corner of Castlegate—the Justice or Thieves Port (*see* **area 9**), so named
from its site on the street leading to the seat of the Justiciar's Circuit Courts beside Castle
Hill; or from the thieves, sentenced to be hanged, passing through this port to Heading
Hill.[17] Repairs to the port were effected during the sixteenth century. Its removal was
ordered in 1769 but, because its west wall formed the gable of a house that encroached on
the south side of the street, it was not finally demolished until 1787.[18] The Gallowgate
Port (Area 1) (sometimes called Calsie or Causey Port) was the most northerly port
controlling movement between New Aberdeen and Old Aberdeen and the north. By 1518
this was considered to be an ancient port, and it was decorated with the royal arms.[19] At
its demolition, sometime between 1769 and 1778,[20] its site had long been on Port Hill. It
is possible, however, that in earlier medieval times the port may have been positioned
further south, and that it was gradually moved further north in response to town
expansion—as may be witnessed in other towns.[21] Upperkirkgate Port or Schoolhill Port
(Area 3) stood on Schoolhill, just within the mill burn. By the time of its demolition a
gallery or room had been constructed above it.[22] This gallery may have been erected as
early as 1585. The port and gallery were purchased by the town council in 1793 for
£140;[23] the last remaining town port was demolished by 1794.[24]

growth of trade

As well as serving to exclude outsiders in time of plague, the ports protected the burgh's market privileges by preventing the illegal import of produce to the market, with the intention of avoiding the payment of tolls. Aberdeen was well situated to become a flourishing market town. It stood on one of the main land routes to the north and north-east of the country.[25] This and its harbour provided two assets from which exchange might develop rapidly, and a town emerge.

The growth of towns was inextricably linked with trade, and Aberdeen must have been an established trading centre by the reign of David I (1124–53). Although evidence of internal and overseas trade in the period before the twelfth century is slight, it is not unrealistic to conclude that it had probably never totally died out during the Dark Ages; and there does seem to be an indication that the latter part of the eleventh century saw a resurgence. According to her contemporary biographer, Queen Margaret, the wife of Malcolm Canmore (1057–1093), encouraged foreign merchants into Scotland;[26] and it is known that in the last decades of the century Scotland was trading with both England and Flanders.[27] Moreover, an assize that has been attributed to the reign of David I suggests that, even by the time of Malcolm Canmore, fixed customs dues had been set on hides for export.[28]

There is little doubt that Aberdeen was one of the participants in this commercial reawakening. As early as the reign of Alexander I (1107–24), it was one of only three trading centres recorded north of the Forth; and it was considerably further north than the other two, Inverkeithing and Perth, which in itself meant that Aberdeen had the potential to dominate trade in the northern parts.[29] This is reinforced by a grant made by William the Lion, c 1180, to his burgesses at Aberdeen, Moray and north of the Mounth. This stated that they should enjoy their free hanse as they did in the time of David I—a specific reference to the existence of settlements of foreign and native traders and an established trade in the first half of the twelfth century.[30] Moreover, by 1136 the bishop of Aberdeen was the recipient of an important concession: the grant of the tithes of all ships coming to Aberdeen.[31] This favouring of the bishopric of Aberdeen indicates not merely the crown's desire to grant financial assistance, but more importantly confirms that the haven of Aberdeen was familiar to, and well frequented by, both seamen and merchants.

Aberdeen was, then, a flourishing trading township by the early decades of the twelfth century. Since it could not have burst on the mercantile scene in a matter of a few years, its origins must therefore lie in the previous century, or earlier.

site of the original settlement

One of the major uncertainties about early Aberdeen is the location of the first urban nucleus. Some local historians have suggested that the original settlement was in the area later called the Green (*see* **area 10**).[32] This is based largely on two factors: the belief in a royal palace situated in the Green and later gifted to the Trinitarians;[33] and the site of St Nicholas Parish Church (Area 7) near the Green and outwith the medieval town ports. No documentary evidence, however, supports the existence of a royal residence in this area. Even if the monarchs' visits had been sufficiently frequent to merit a permanent royal lodging, a more defensible spot would probably have been selected than the site of the Trinitarian House. Nor need the extra-urban situation of St Nicholas Church necessarily imply that it was intended to serve a community centred outside the town ports. The siting of a parish church outwith the main urban settlement is not unknown; similar examples are to be found in Dundee and Crail. Indeed, a parish church was not of necessity an urban parish church: rural parishes might pre-date urban growth—such as the parish of St Cuthbert's, out of which the urban parish of St Giles was carved at the time of the foundation of the king's burgh of Edinburgh.

Arguments *against* the Green as the site of the first settlement are that the area was marshy and water-logged at the confluence of the Denburn and the Dee, and consequently unfavourable to building. Moreover, archaeological excavations and observations at the western end of the Green, at 2–12 Rennie's Wynd and 67–71 Green (*see* **area 10**), indicate that this area was highly susceptible to flooding: no pre-urban or early urban settlement was revealed and archaeologists concluded that, although parts of the west end of the Green were in use by the end of the twelfth century, it could be discounted as an early centre of intense activity.[34] This would seem to suggest that original settlement lay elsewhere, perhaps in the Broadgate/Castlegate area—the market centre of the medieval town. Another argument against the Green is that it became the focus for two important orders_the Trinitarians and the Carmelites. Since religious orders tended to place their houses on the periphery of a settlement, this again implies that the Green was merely a suburb to the main nucleus of early settlement. The Trinitarian and Carmelite houses, however, were thirteenth-century foundations; it is possible, therefore, that they were established on marginal urban sites if they were founded *after* the focus of urban settlement had moved to the Broadgate/Castlegate area.

Archaeological research indicates that tofts were being laid out for the first time in the Upperkirkgate in the mid twelfth century (*see* **area 3**).[35] Perhaps this is partial evidence for the movement of the original settlement: the original site may have been in the Green, not at the water-logged western end, but rather at the foot of St Katherine's Hill. It offered a far better supply of water than the Castlegate/Broadgate nucleus; St Katherine's Hill was as readily defensible as Castle Hill and might, hypothetically, have been topped with some primitive fortification in early times, providing some form of protection to the settlement at its western slope; and St Nicholas Church or a predecessor could have acted as a religious focus. Although no archaeological excavation has been possible in Back Wynd (Area 7), the work which has been undertaken in the area, and the street layout, suggest that the eastern end of the Green, skirting the base of St Katherine's Hill eastwards towards Shiprow and northwards up Putachieside to the church, would have been an ideal site for early settlement. Further, St Katherine's Hill overlooks the junction of Putachie Burn and Denburn at the highest navigable point of the estuary. There was one disadvantage: lack of space for expansion. To the south and west lay water or water-logged terrain and, to the east, the steep slope of St Katherine's Hill. Hence, possibly, the move to higher, drier land in the Castlegate/Broadgate region.

Such theories are highly speculative and confirmation of one or other hypothesis about the site of the first settlement in Aberdeen must await further archaeological investigation. An assessment of the eastern end of the Green might have yielded important evidence, whether positive or negative, but the potential in this area has been largely destroyed.[36] The balance of the evidence available at present, however, perhaps slightly favours the view that the original settlement may have been at the eastern end of the Green, at the foot of St Katherine's Hill.

water supply

The situation of water supplies would also have greatly influenced the position of the burgh. Burns and small lochs, the essential supply of domestic and industrial water and also a natural source of power, were patterned by the distinctive geological characteristics of both New and Old Aberdeen (*see* pp 5–6). Meltwater from the final stages of the last Ice Age resulted in the formation of gravel and sand mounds between the Dee and Don estuaries. These mounds, reinforced by sand dunes and ridges to the east, proved major obstacles to the free flow of water down the natural easterly slope to the shore of the North Sea. In consequence, small lochans and marshy areas formed between and around the mounds, and streams were diverted from an easterly direction to flow south, parallel to the North Sea coast.[37] In the Middle Ages the major water supplies for New Aberdeen were, as a result, the lower Denburn and the Loch of New Aberdeen (in Areas 1, 2 and 6), reinforced by streams running to the west of St Katherine's Hill.

The two major feeders of the medieval loch were the Westburn or Gilcomston Burn, which rose in Mastrick, and Spital or Froghall Burn, which had its source at the west side of Spital Hill, at the present Sunnyside Road. It has been argued that these two burns were diverted in the early Middle Ages down the east side of Guest Row (Areas 4 and 7) before houses had been built, to run a mill at the foot of Broad Street and Guest Row, then pass under Exchequer Row (Areas 8 and 11) and down the steep slope to the Denburn, which then ran along the line of present Virginia Street (Area 9).[38] If this were the case, such a water system would have provided an invaluable supply to the Castlegate area of New Aberdeen, which had no such natural resources. The evidence, however, is based solely on nineteenth-century archaeological information. No current archaeological work has confirmed this hypothesis. Supporting documentary evidence is likewise lacking. With its two feeder burns cut off by the end of the Middle Ages, the town loch soon dried up. By the seventeenth century geese were feeding in 'the grass of the loch',[39] by 1661 Gordon calls the loch a 'marisch',[40] and Taylor's map in 1773 shows the bed of the loch as dry land called the 'Lochlands'.

The fifteenth-century Sasine Registers of Aberdeen hold crucial evidence on the water courses near the Trinitarian House and lower Green region, and in particular on the 'common torrent' which led from the 'aqueduct of the mills',[41] which may possibly be synonymous with the Putachie; and on the 'two torrents' that led to the Trinitarian House and the lower mill.[42] The Carmelite House (Area 10) was supplied with water by lead piping[43] and may also have used this same source of water. References, for example, to the Putachie Stream are rare in primary sources. One explanation appears in a disposition of 1741 when a Temple tenement is described as having as its western boundary 'the burn sometime called the mill burn and now Putachies burn'.[44] When this same tenement had been described in 1636,[45] for instance, as having a boundary as 'millburn' there was no indication that this was indeed the Putachie. All references to the 'mill burn', however, are not synonymous with this stream. It is clear that two, if not more, branches of the same water course were termed the 'mill burn'. A systematic assessment of the existing documentary source material could result in a precise plotting of this water course.

What is significant for Aberdeen is that the major water supply for the town passed to the west of Guest Row and St Katherine's Hill. In consequence, the majority of crafts which required water power were focused at the west end of the town. The dyers, or litsters, for example, congregated around the Netherkirkgate, Putachieside and the east end of the Green. This continued into modern times and from 1659 the litsters maintained their hall on the lands that had once been owned by Arbroath Abbey, on the south side of the Netherkirkgate.[46] The schedule drawn up in 1800 to assess properties which would be affected by the proposed new south entry to Aberdeen (Union Street), and its accompanying detailed map of 1798, indicate not only the continuing importance of this water course but also the presence of at least one dyer in Putachieside.[47]

As the medieval town expanded the need for a better water supply became urgent. The inhabitants supplemented their water by rain collected in water butts and from wells sunk in the backlands of tofts and closes. Probably each of the friaries (in Areas 2, 4, and 10) and St Thomas's Hospital (Area 7) had their own draw-wells.[48] Communal wells were also in use, for example, the Well of Spa, situated to the west of the present-day Spa Street and the Thieves Brig Well, which was sunk after 1558 when the town council granted a licence to dig to one William Robertson and his neighbours, provided it was surrounded by a protecting wall of stone and lime.[49] There was a demand for water from millers and dyers, and also other crafts such as fullers, tanners, smiths and brewers. In due course such industrial use brought contamination, and in 1632 the town council minuted that the springs, streams, water channels and mill lades were 'filthillie defyllit and corruptit not onlie be gutteris daylie rynning in the burne, but also be litsteris and the washing of clothes and abwssing of the water in sindrie partis, with wther sorts of uncleanness'.[50] Proposals were made to bring spring water into the burgh, but nothing was achieved. A further attempt to pipe pure water to the town was made in 1682; but it was not until the eighteenth century that water was finally piped into the central areas of the town, and even this proved not fully adequate.[51] A main 'fountain', however, was erected in Castlegate in 1706, fed from lead pipes from Carden's Well, surmounted by a temporary wooden figure which was replaced by a lead statue, 'the Mannie'. In 1852 this was moved to the Green, but it was once more re-erected in the twentieth century, in the Castlegate where it still stands (Area 8).[52] In 1782 Aberdeen was visited by Douglas while on his tour of the east coast of Scotland. He deemed that 'the town is plentifully supplied with excellent water brought in lead pipes from springs about a mile to the west ward'.[53]

mills

A detailed analysis of references to water supplies has yet to be carried out, but some indications of the courses of streams comes from the positioning of mills. The earliest extant documentary evidence of a mill that has been noted is of one driven by a stream named the Holburn or Rubislaw.[54] This was later supplemented by a further mill, and was outwith the town, to the west, situated to the east of the present Holburn Street at the modern Justice Mill Lane, and would have been approached from medieval New Aberdeen via the Green and Windmill Brae (Area 10). The town, however, had the facility of a meal mill within its confines by the fourteenth century and this may have been one of the 'town's mills' in need of repair in 1407.[55] It was sited in what became Flourmill Brae (which is now below St Nicholas Centre) and was to become known as the Upper Mill (Areas 3 and 7). This is seen clearly on Gordon's map of 1661 **figure 6**, along with the Nether Mill which had been constructed before 1525 to the north of the Trinitarian House (Area 10), and perhaps as early as 1459, when a reference to a 'higher' mill would imply the existence of another mill lower down the water course.[56]

A further mill, the Mid Mill in the Green (Area 7), was to use the same water power from 1619.[57] On a line with present Union Street, it functioned as a meal mill, and later a malt mill, until 1798 when plans were made for its removal for the creation of Union Street. The Upper and Nether Mills, however, continued to work until 1865.

What is not clear, however, is the precise line of the water-course that led to these three mills. By 1438 the Denburn was tapped where Gilcomston Dam was later constructed. This course was to work several mills and industrial works until the nineteenth century, but its original function was to supplement the supply of water from the Spital Burn and the Westburn in the regions of the present Maberley Street. From here it passed to Loch Street, along which line it ran as a mill dam separated from the loch by a bank of earth.[58] The mill dam then passed over Upperkirkgate near the port, but whether to the east or west is not clear. Secondary and cartographic sources are unreliable on this point, and no direct archaeological evidence has so far been discovered.

Primary source material indicates that the mill dam or lade passed for at least some of the length of the west end of tofts on Guest Row. Provost Skene's House (Area 4), as well as others on the west side of Guest Row, is described on several occasions as having a western boundary of 'the mill lade'.[59] Whether part of the water course continued the full length of the back tofts of Guest Row to Netherkirkgate or was entirely diverted westwards to supply the Upper Mill could probably be established by a thorough search of both contemporary and later burgh sasines. Equally interesting would be a clarification of the source of the Putachie Burn. It has been claimed that this stream started as a spring at the north end of the street which consequently became called Putachieside.[60] It is, however, possible that this small course, still clearly visible as late as 1773 on Taylor's map of Aberdeen, was a minor offshoot of the important complex water course on the west side of St Katherine's Hill.

the twelfth- to thirteenth-century burgh and its municipal organisation

Although no original documentation has survived, it appears that Aberdeen was granted the status of a king's burgh during the reign of David I, for, as indicated above, a charter dated *c* 1180 and issued by William I, the grandson of David, confers to the 'burgesses' of Aberdeen all the privileges enjoyed in David's reign.[61] The advantages of burghal status were many, but basically two-fold. First, while initially under the supervision of the king's chosen officer, Aberdeen, like other burghs held by the crown, was to develop a certain autonomy in the conduct of its affairs, although largely conforming to an accepted common mercantile and burgh law.[62] There was much commonality of burghal custom throughout northern France, England and Scotland. Laws were borrowed from Breteuil and Newcastle; and the privileges of Perth were explicitly granted to Aberdeen. The significance for Aberdeen was that this adopted burgh law was a common base which could be adapted or improved to suit the needs of the community of Aberdeen. The town's affairs were conducted by an alderman and four bailies,[63] probably with the support of the more substantial burgesses though a burgh court and/or council. The use of a burgh seal, the symbol of the community, by the mid thirteenth century, would also indicate some degree of self-government.[64] By 1319 the burgh was granted a feu-ferme charter, one of the first of its kind documented in Scotland.[65] By this grant, the community was placed formally and in perpetuity in receipt of all the revenues from the common good: revenues from the burgh courts; the fishings (which were south of the harbour); and multures (payments to use the town mills—the windmill to the north of the town and the water-powered mills, market tolls, rentals and so on). What is significant is not so much the actual grant of feu-ferme status, for it may merely have been setting on a formal footing an already existing practice, but the indication that the burgh's financial organisation was of sufficient sophistication to deal with the collection of such revenues and the payment, in exchange, to the crown, of £213.6.8 per annum. By the time that the burgh court records of Aberdeen are extant (1317 and 1398–1407, the earliest in Scotland), the burgh had developed an efficient municipal organisation functioning through three head courts and more frequent lesser courts. As well as the alderman and bailies, it had a common council of between twelve and twenty-four members and minor officers such as liners (whose responsibility it was to measure burgh plots), ale- and meat-tasters, sergeants, treasurers and masters of the kirk work.[66]

Secondly, of equal, if not greater, importance were the benefits that accrued to the town as a market for internal and overseas trade once burgh status had been confirmed. Between 1187 and 1203 Aberdeen burgesses were freed from paying tolls on their goods throughout the kingdom.[67] The reign of Alexander II (1214–49), in particular, saw an extension of the town's trading rights. In 1222 a weekly Sunday market was established; and a woollen cloth market was reserved to Aberdeen burgesses (except between Ascension Day and Lammas, the summer months).[68] This market became the commercial focus for the surrounding fertile hinterland. Not only did the burgh benefit from the produce, such as corn, barley, malt, fish and cattle, brought in for sale at its market and the consequent payment of tolls for the privilege; but the neighbouring villages and agricultural settlements proved, in their turn, to be customers for the surplus and manufactured goods of the town craftsmen. By 1273, a further important concession was granted - the right to hold an annual fair (in the fortnight after Trinity).[69] Aberdeen could thus become a distribution point for the rural hinterland and, in addition, was also in a position to attract trade from further afield. So favoured was this fair that in 1289 an appeal was made by the provost and burgesses of Banff that Aberdeen should be permitted to hold its fair fortnightly and unmolested, since it had been obstructed by burgesses of Montrose 'to the no small prejudice and injury of the foresaid burgh of Aberdeen and indeed of the whole northern province'.[70] By the fourteenth century, Aberdeen had emerged as one of the four wealthiest and most important burghs in Scotland.

With its port on the fringe of a hinterland rich in tradeable commodities such as wool, woolfells and hides, and its fishings supplying salmon and other fish, Aberdeen exploited not merely local commerce but also overseas trade through its established guild merchant.[71] Burgesses travelled to England and the Low Countries, importing from them wines, spices and luxury items, and into the Baltic for such commodities as flax, timber, iron and, at times, grain. In exchange not only was fish exported[72] but, most importantly, wool, woolfells and hides. Scottish wool imported into St Omer by the late thirteenth century was differentiated by port of origin. Significantly, although Perth's wool was rated as the best, that of Aberdeen, Berwick and Montrose was regarded as the next most desirable.[73] Although there is little archaeological material which can be construed as direct evidence of trade, a flavour of European and wider contacts is present from the thirteenth century onwards in a range of imported pottery and a few exotic objects such as a piece of silk and a spindle whorl of elephant ivory.[74] Some of the fragments of woollen cloth found during excavations in the burgh were almost certainly woven in the Low Countries/Netherlands, possibly from Scottish wool.[75]

the street layout established

The town's wealth manifested itself in the physical appearance of the burgh, and by the fourteenth century the basic street-pattern had been established. The focal point for the townspeople was Castlegate where the market was held. (Some argue for an earlier market in Broadgate: *see below*.) The main settlement seems to have been centred on the market area, to the north up Broadgate, Gallowgate and Upperkirkgate; on Netherkirkgate; to the south down Exchequer Row and Shiprow, leading to the Quayhead (Area 11), and westwards into the Green; and eastwards down Futty Wynd (Area 9) to the little fishing suburb of Futty. Perhaps the most imposing architectural features of the town, apart from the castle, were the main ecclesiastical establishments: St Nicholas Parish Church (Area 7), the Carmelite and Trinitarian friaries in the Green (Area 10) and the Dominican friary on Schoolhill (Area 2), the extension of Upperkirkgate. All were the recipients of donations and the good works of burgesses. Much of Aberdeen's prosperity came from wealthy merchants and craftsmen. Luxury crafts were starting to be in demand in Aberdeen and there was a resident goldsmith by the 1280s.[76] A mint was established in the fourteenth century which probably implies a fair level of commercial traffic in Aberdeen.[77]

The wealthier townspeople tended to live in the more valuable property, and there is some evidence that rentals were higher in the Castlegate, Gallowgate and Exchequer Row area (although rentals might vary, in Exchequer Row, for example, from 16s 8d to 60s). This would conform with the pattern of other burghs, where property values were greatest near the market. Sir John Rutherfurd, for example, paid £100 in 1485 for two Gallowgate properties, which may not be seen as a cheap investment.[78] The majority of houses were timber-built. Excavation has produced evidence of a number of post-and-wattle structures in the backlands (*see* **area 3**: 42 St Paul Street) and examples, in a frontage context, of sill-beam construction (Area 3: 45–47 Gallowgate). Apart from ecclesiastical buildings, the earliest archaeological evidence, to date, of stone walls (as opposed to stone foundations supporting a timber superstructure) comes from a building dated broadly to the fifteenth to seventeenth century (Area 3: 42 St Paul Street). Documentary sources, however, indicate the presence of at least one stone house in Gallowgate by 1317.[79] Normally, roofing was probably of heather, straw or rush thatch, although there is little direct archaeological evidence of this; and, in due course, on more substantial buildings, pottery tiles, sometimes brightly coloured, were used and have been found in archaeological excavations. Wooden houses were susceptible to fire—a threat throughout the Middle Ages. Such was the devastation caused by fire in 1326, for example, that the burgh was excused ten years feu-ferme payments.[80] Window glass was rare, windows being shuttered or covered with matting during night-time or inclement weather, though glass became more common in the better quality burgh houses in the fifteenth century. In 1399, a contract was made with two Aberdeen masons for windows and doors, although archaeological finds suggest that a large proportion of glass was imported, perhaps as raw glass.[81] Forestairs giving access from outside to the upper storey of a house also became a more frequent feature. Appended to the fronts of houses lining the streets, near the market area, were wooden booths where merchants and craftsmen sold their wares.

Some craftsmen and poorer indwellers, however, pursued their trades and made their homes in the less desirable and cheaper areas of the town—often in the backlands. Tofts or burgage plots were measured out by the official town liners. On most of the tofts a dwelling would be built on the street frontage. Behind ran a long rig or strip of land, initially intended to supply home-grown produce or graze domestic animals, such as pigs. As pressure for space increased, however, these backlands were developed for dwelling and industrial purposes. In most cases such backland property was of considerably poorer quality than frontage dwellings. This has been confirmed by excavations in St Paul Street (the backlands of Upperkirkgate) (*see* **area 3**), Queen Street and Broad Street (Area 8).[82] Pressure for space, however, must not be overstressed, even though archaeological evidence would suggest that this was the situation as early as the thirteenth century, and the gradual ribbon development up Gallowgate is an indication of population expansion (in the early fifteenth century, it has been estimated, the population was somewhere between 4,000 and 5,000.)[83] A site at the rear of Broadgate (on present Queen Street; Area 8, Queen Street Midden Area) became a midden in the fourteenth century and, in the 1460s, a large area of land in Broadgate/Gallowgate was given to the Franciscans. Neither case indicates scarcity of land.

The medieval town was one of open spaces and gardens essentially of a rural nature. The friaries were surrounded by cultivated land and orchards. Burgesses not only grew crops on their rigs but also reared animals. Barns and stables, dunghills on the thoroughfares[84] and livestock roaming the streets, with the obvious concomitant nuisance value, were common features. And the townspeople retained close links with the countryside around: hunting and fishing in the hinterland; collecting moss; gathering fruits, berries, fat hen and nettles for food and wattle, turves and heather for thatching; and, for building and fuel, a wood and peat supply was necessary. Much of this would have come from the nearby forest of Stocket **figure 2**, possession of which was given to the town by Robert I (1306–1329),[85] one of the several grants made by this monarch to the town, probably in recompense for support during the Wars of Independence. The burgh's croft territories surrounded the town: the Futty territory to the east, Gallowgate territory to the north and the Denburn territory to the west. By 1300, the individual crofts were being brought together and sold off as units. The burgh's purchase of Rubislaw in 1379, however, provided not only further croft territories but also extra grazing for the burgesses' livestock.[86] The town had a common herdsman by 1399 at latest.[87] Aberdeen, although a thriving urban distribution centre and port, was still very much tied to the country and relied on the rural hinterland for its survival.

prominence of the burgh up to the seventeenth century

Gordon of Rothiemay's map of 1661 **figure 6**, while it may not be accepted as definitive in detail, gives the impression of a town not greatly altered from medieval days. The street pattern remains largely the same, although a few additional thoroughfares are noted. There is very little evidence of repletion (building in the backlands of tofts) and most of the rigs appear still to be gardens. But there had been change in the town. During the late Middle Ages and in the sixteenth and seventeenth centuries, Aberdeen had continued to feel the effects of national politics. The burgh's importance in Scotland had been shown as early as 1296 when Aberdeen's seal was one of six burgh seals to be appended to the ratification of the treaty with France.[88] From the mid fourteenth century, the burgh was not only represented regularly in parliament, but was also of significance to the crown, making an important contribution to national taxation. The town's loyalty to the Scottish crown, exhibited during the Wars of Independence and the invasions of English armies during the fourteenth century, continued in the fifteenth and early sixteenth centuries in active opposition to the English. Aberdeen's contribution to the Flodden campaign in 1513, for example, was twenty spearmen, three horsemen and three horses, at a cost of £200 Scots, as well as a further £1000 raised by the townspeople and individual donations by wealthy burgesses.[89]

Of all the national, political issues that were to have an impact on Aberdeen, the Reformation crisis was one that had a particularly profound effect on the burgh landscape and on the lives of the townspeople. Within the town itself, the conservative establishment headed by the Menzies family remained firmly in control, although its policy on religious

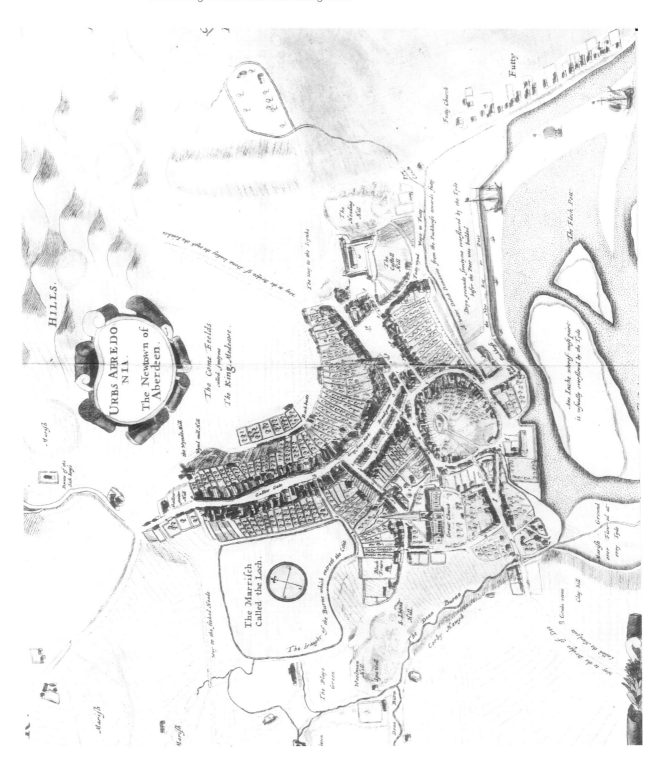

figure 6

New Aberdeen,
Gordon of Rothiemay's
map
1661

issues tended to be ambiguous. There was little support within the burgh for the
Protestant mob of outsiders from Angus and the Mearns that arrived on 4 January 1560,
although the town was unable to prevent the sacking of its friaries. The burgh council
took into its safekeeping the ecclesiastical vestments and treasures from the parish church
during the Reformation crisis, but it also sent representatives from the different shades of
opinion within it to the Reformation parliament in August 1560, at which time it also
appointed a Protestant minister.[90] By 1562, some of the ornaments of St Nicholas Church
were offered for sale and a kirk session belatedly set up. Yet when the Regent Morton
visited the burgh in 1574, he found that what was one of Scotland's most impressive
parish churches retained the essential outlines of a Catholic place of worship, with organ,
choir stalls, choir screen and reredos still intact.[91]

The following century saw Aberdeen's long involvement in the civil wars of Scotland, sparked off by the town council's refusal in March 1638 to sign the National Covenant. Occupied by looting armies on a number of occasions, subject to exacting taxations for the quartering of such troops and fines for opposition to the Covenanting cause, the town became the sparring ring for both Royalists and Covenanters until 1646. Gordon of Rothiemay wrote:

> *Quhilst the civill warrs did overrun all, ther was no citie in Scotland which did suffer more hurt than Aberdeen did, nor oftener, aither cessing, quartering, plundering, burning or slaughtering the inhabitants ... whence it came to passe that the citie, which floorished in wealth and trade, wes miserable impoverished.*[92]

Aberdeen, however, had not seen the last of occupying forces. In 1651, General Monck's troops arrived, but their stay was marked by none of the ravages typical of the 1640s. On Castle Hill (*see* **area 5**), a bastioned fort was erected using stones from the Cathedral of St Machar and the Bishop's Palace in Old Aberdeen. A section of what may have been the ramparts remains standing on the south side of the hill.

The town and its inhabitants also fell prey to less dramatic but equally insidious enemies - disease and fire. Standards of cleanliness and sanitation remained primitive throughout the later Middle Ages. Most refuse—personal, domestic and industrial—was still dumped in middens in backlands or in the streets, including all the waste products of the skinners' and furriers' crafts. Animals were free to root amongst the tips, and contaminated water in the gutters might readily flow into supplies of water for washing or drinking. Epidemics of disease were rife in spite of efforts by the council: middens were to be cleared once a year; a town 'scaffyngir' was appointed in 1494 and for this a tax of 1d was raised upon each house and merchant's or craftsman's booth;[93] and serious attempts were made to clean up the town for the visit of Queen Margaret in 1511.[94] The arrival of the Black Death in 1350 did not have a major impact on the town, but there were to be regular outbreaks of plague—in 1401, 1498, 1500, 1501, 1514, 1530, 1538, 1545, 1546 and in 1608—and burgh routine was sufficiently upset between August 1500 and January 1501 that no records were kept on account of the severity of the outbreak.[95] Cholera, typhus, amoebic dysentery, smallpox and tuberculosis, as well as other diseases, took their regular toll, as did leprosy. The need for quarantine measures in cases both of leprosy and plague was understood. Special areas, for example, were set out for washing clothes during the plague and in 1499 the Aberdeen authorities forbade trading with 'north partis' until north-east Scotland was free of plague.[96] A leper house (*see* **area 14**) was established on the Spital, outwith the precincts of the town, but leprosy was to lose its virulence in the seventeenth century. Not so the plague. In 1646 the pest or plague was moving northwards. All ports, and all ships entering the harbour of Aberdeen, were watched. Three gibbets were set up:

> *ane at the mercat cross, ane other at the brig of Dee, and the third at the haven mouth, that in case ony infectit person arrive or repair by sea or land to the burgh, or in case ony indweller of the burgh receive, house or harbour, or give meat or drink to the infectit person or persons, the man be hangit and the woman drownit.*[97]

In spite of such stringent measures, the disease still attacked the burgh and attempts were made to isolate the infected in huts which served as shelters on Woolmanhill, on the site of the present City Hospital and elsewhere on the links. Those who died were burnt or buried in mass graves, outwith the town (*see* **area 12**, York Place),[98] and it is probable that one quarter of the town's populace perished in this way.[99]

Fire was still a constant threat, with a predominance of timber houses with thatched roofs. In spite of this, the replacement of stone for wood and slate for thatch was a slow process. Gordon maintained that 'buildings of the toune are of stone and lyme, rigged above, covered with slaits, mostly of thrie or four stories hight, some of them higher'.[100] He was, however, speaking only of the better quality housing. There was indeed a stone house in the burgh by the early fourteenth century, but as late as 1448 a property in the Exchequer Row was described as a 'sclate hous', thus implying that slates were not the norm.[101] A prestigious house on the south side of Castlegate, Menzies of Pitfoddels' lodging, was replaced in stone as late as 1535, the timber predecessor having burned down in 1529, and the Earl Marischal's town-house, further east, built *c* 1540, was probably the first stone structure on that site.[102] Thatching was in common use even in the seventeenth century. In 1613, 23 shillings had to be paid 'for repairing the gramer schole, the thak thairof being blauin off'.[103] Indeed, it was not until 1716 that thatching was prohibited and as late as 1731, after a major fire in the Gallowgate, that timber houses were forbidden.[104]

the later medieval and early modern burgh

material prosperity and the regulation of trade

In spite of the hazards to life, the burgh continued to prosper commercially in the later Middle Ages. One of the primary functions of the market in Castlegate was the provision of foodstuffs and raw materials and its service as an outlet centre for the surpluses and manufactured goods of the town. There is evidence of trade resulting from the crafts of coopers, goldsmiths, silversmiths and tailors.[105] The burgh records reveal a town council which consistently regulated trade, theoretically for the good of the burgh community. Officers were appointed to enforce burgh statutes and fines were imposed by the council and guild merchant on those 'outsiders' who sought to encroach on their privileges and on those who used unfair trading practices, such as forestalling (the purchase of goods before they reached market, thus avoiding the payment of toll) or regrating (purchase in bulk to sell at an advantageous time when prices were high). Periodic attempts were made to control the sale of fish at Futty, which was carried on without permission and proved detrimental to the burgh market. Prices were fixed and quality maintained by inspection; for example, in the 1440s ale was to be sold at 4d and 6d a gallon.[106] The price statutes, moreover, give clear evidence of a price inflation in the burgh market between 1435 and 1531. Debased coinage was also to have an impact: the price of bread doubled and mutton more than doubled in price.[107] These statutes were waived in times of food shortage, however, for the common good of the town.

But Aberdeen's market cast its net well beyond the confines of the burgh. In the early Middle Ages, it seems that the burgh had become the centre of an important regional trade. The records of the late medieval town indicate that Aberdeen maintained and even enhanced its firm grip on the commerce of the north-east, consolidating its position at the end of the fifteenth century and the beginning of the sixteenth at the expense of other towns in the region. In 1485 Aberdeen's percentage share of burgh taxation within the north-east was 52.6 per cent compared to Inverness at 19.7 per cent. By 1535, this had risen to 62.8 per cent compared to Inverness's 11.2 per cent.[108] In 1502, the town council gained royal permission to fine all those who traded outwith the burgh gates, thereby avoiding town regulations and taxes. Seventeen years later, special licences were instituted, enabling those merchants who wished to do so, to trade in the north-east, with the sanction of the authorities.[109] Whether or not this system was in fact enforceable is uncertain. But Gordon of Rothiemay's comment in 1661 is significant, even if exaggerated: 'market tounes villedges and hamlets of the shyres and countrey nearest neighbouring to Aberdeine ... are ... subject to thame, that without the licence of Aberdeen they dare nather trade in merchandise ather by sea or land'.[110]

There is firm evidence, moreover, that Aberdeen served as an entrepôt for the north-east. Elgin and Banff, for example, sent much of their salmon to Aberdeen for re-export to other areas of Scotland and overseas, as did at least two north-east barons. By the late Middle Ages, the town had trading contacts with Orkney along the length of the east coast— with Caithness, Dundee, Perth, St Andrews, Dysart, Leith, Edinburgh and Berwick on Tweed. Of these, Leith was the outstandingly dominant port. Foreign goods were then retailed from Aberdeen to such centres as Montrose, Elgin, Forres and Orkney, to the profit of the burgh, and in particular of merchant families such as the Menzies and Rutherfurds in the early sixteenth century.[111] The presence of such a wealthy, landed elite within the town also increased demand for the goods and services of craftsmen, and for better quality housing in the urban centre, all of which promoted a balanced burgh economy.

Of considerable significance within this economy was the export trade in salmon and dried fish developed by merchant burgesses. Robert Blinseile, provost of Aberdeen, for example, exported salmon and 'fynans' to the Low Countries through the agency of Andrew Haliburton, Scottish Conservator there at the end of the fifteenth century.[112] Aberdeen had long benefited from favoured terms governing its fish trade. In 1323, King Robert I had granted to the town freedom from payment of duty on ale and red and white fish.[113] Aberdeen's own fish, as well as that of the other north-east burghs, was exported throughout Scotland and to England and further afield. The extent of Aberdeen's export trade in fish and other commodities abroad, however, must not be exaggerated. Those merchants who traded overseas were a very small minority; and even this minority was largely dominated by eleven elite families.[114] As late as the 1620s, there were perhaps only 300 active traders and of these a mere seventy-five were in any one year involved in overseas trade[115] in a population that has been estimated as then between 7,500 and 10,000.[116]

Aberdeen's wealth did not rely solely on the success of its merchants. The skills of craftsmen were an essential adjunct to a balanced society, and by the late Middle Ages there had emerged a small group of craftsmen capable of challenging in terms of wealth the dominant merchant group. By the middle of the fifteenth century at least 150 craftsmen were already of sufficient wealth to be assessed for burgh taxation, and 13.5 per cent of the entry into the guild merchant came from candidates of craft status. By the first half of the sixteenth century, this percentage had risen to 23.3 per cent.[117] For 1587, there is recorded both a general tax and a customs tax assessed on burghs. The first reflected wealth accruing from various sources, the second purely from trade. Aberdeen's percentage assessment for the general tax was 9.17 per cent of the Scottish burghs' total, whereas when assessed purely on its customs returns, the Aberdeen burgh share was less, at 7.20 per cent. There may here be signs that the flow of overseas trade through Aberdeen's port, while increasing, was not keeping pace with the rise enjoyed by some of its main competitors. The guild court did complain in 1590 that Aberdeen merchants were frequenting Leith overmuch and it is possible that they were using other ports for their business at the expense of their own burgh. Alternatively, Aberdeen's thriving trade in salmon could have been greater than has been thought. This would not be reflected in the 1587 figures because of the burgh's commercial privileges in this particular trade. This 'hidden' unrecorded trade could have been further supplemented if nobles exporting through Aberdeen also paid no custom. There were fluctuations, but Aberdeen's share of customs revenue during the period 1460–1499, 11.73 per cent of the national trade, sets it as the second wealthiest burgh, compared with Edinburgh's 59.39 per cent, Dundee's 6.45 per cent and Perth's 2.86 per cent. For the period 1535–1594, based on the average of total burgh taxation, Aberdeen would rank third—at 9.02 per cent—following Edinburgh's 26.81 per cent and Dundee's 11.54 per cent.[118] In 1495 a levy on burghs resulted in an assessment for Aberdeen of £200 compared with rival Montrose's £50.[119]

Fluctuations in trade were to continue into the seventeenth century. Between 1605 and 1610 and between 1615 and 1623/4 both imports and exports rose. This increased wealth manifested itself on the townscape: two mills operated by the tide were constructed and the town quay was extended eastwards. A further period of expansion came between 1630 and 1638, particularly with trade to Flanders, and resulted in the building of a slaughterhouse in 1631, the founding of a craft hospital in 1632, the refurbishment of the

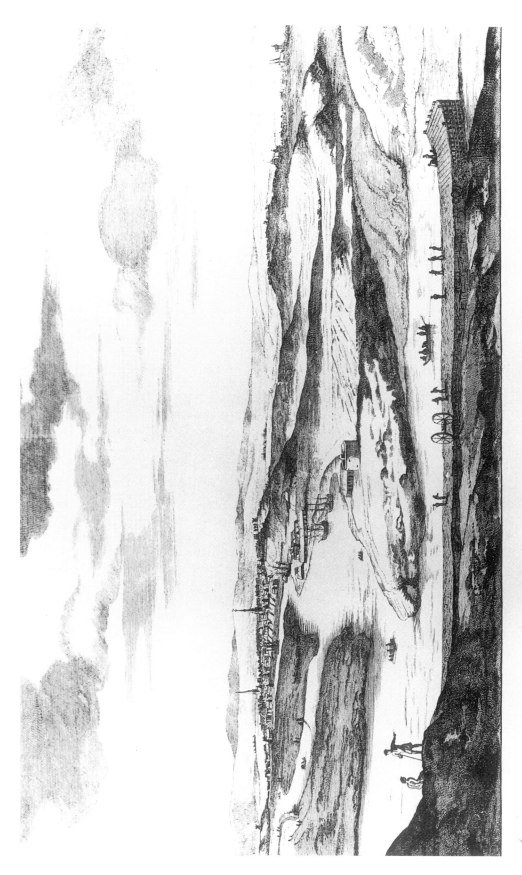

Tacis Civitatis Novæ ABREDONIÆ ut a propugnaculo Blockhous dito aspicitur . New ABERDENE from the Block house ,

figure 7

John Slezer's vignette
of New Aberdeen
c 1693

Greyfriars Church (*see* **area 4**), the provision of a new water supply in 1633, the setting up of a correction house in 1636 (thus giving the name to Correction Wynd: Area 7) and the construction of a packhouse, where food could be weighed and duties levied, in 1634.[120] The latter half of the seventeenth century might be considered as one of comparative decline. The Covenanting Wars had a profound effect on the burgh economy with disruption of trade and normal commercial practice. The export of plaiding (a coarse, twilled cloth made from carded wool), for example, which had begun in the 1580s, peaked in 1639 when 121,000 ells left Aberdeen for the Netherlands, the Baltic and the north of France. Thereafter decline set in, until 1750 saw the total demise of Aberdeenshire cloth.[121] Aberdeen's percentage of total burgh taxation of 8 per cent in 1601 held firm until 1635. Thereafter, there was a steady decline until in 1697 its share was a mere 4.5 per cent. Other factors, social, industrial and commercial, may have come into play,[122] but Glasgow's impact on the commercial scene must be taken into account. Its emergence as a wealthy trading burgh had roots firmly set in the sixteenth century,[123] but its effect on the traditionally oriented east coast burghs was not truly felt until the seventeenth century. Provincial centres, such as Dundee and Aberdeen, were simply not in a good enough geographical position to capitalise on the newly developing trade routes, in particular those to the Americas.

Aberdeen and its surrounding rural hinterland, which produced much of the plaids and stockings that the town exported, were also hit harshly by the famines of 1695 and 1699. The north-east of Scotland suffered greatly and Aberdeenshire faced starvation on a massive scale. In spite of such measures as poor relief, expulsion of beggars, who flocked to the town for assistance, and attempts by the town council to control distribution and the price of food, the town faced a fatal crisis. Mortality, infertility and emigration reduced the population of Aberdeen parish from approximately 7,100 in 1695 to 5,600 in 1700.[124] Although Aberdeen itself was to recover by 1755 to a population of about 10,700, the population of Aberdeenshire, as a whole, had not regained the 1695 level more than half a century after the famine crisis ended.[125]

the eighteenth century onwards

Paterson's map of 1746 suggests that Aberdeen had changed little from the days of Gordon of Rothiemay, other than the purchase in 1679 of the lands of Gilcomston by the town council—the first signs of a westwards expansion. A number of mills—lint, meal and flour—had also been established, which is a fair reflection of the strength of the local economy (*see also* **gazetteer**).[126] By the second half of the eighteenth century considerable change was being effected on the townscape, some evidenced in Milne's map published in 1789. Within the burgh new industries were developing (*see* **gazetteer**) and the port was to undergo vast expansion. In the burgh centre old timber buildings were being replaced with more substantial granite constructions. Loanhead was the first local granite quarry to open in 1730. The central building of Gordon's Hospital was built of this stone. Rubislaw Quarry opened in 1741 and Dyce in 1766.[127] New streets were also changing the character of the town as increased prosperity brought material improvements, North Street, Belmont Street, Virginia Street and Marischal Street being the most notable. All were precursors of the extensive nineteenth-century road modifications that not only reflected the role of modern Aberdeen in the Scottish economy, but also, with the construction of Union Street, removed many traces of the central core of the town. This trend was continued with twentieth-century shopping malls, consumer centres and blocks of flats. Some remnants of the Middle Ages are still in evidence, but the modern city has to an extent obliterated the small but important medieval burgh of New Aberdeen.

notes

1   Area numbers in parentheses: refer to the relevant area in **area by area assessment**.
2   Simpson, *Hidden History*, 23.
3   Robertson, 22, 23.
4   *Ibid*, 24.
5   Murray, J C, 'The Archaeological Evidence' in Smith, *New Light*, 13, 16.
6   *RRS*, i, 80.
7   Duncan, 193.
8   *Ibid*, 468.
9   *Aberdeen Council Register*, i, 37; i, 123.
10   Murray, J C, 246–7.
11   *Ibid*, 247.
12   *Aberdeen Description*, 9–10.
13   MS *Aberdeen Council Register*, v 2, 600; v 2, 663 also refers to town defences.
14   MS *Aberdeen Council Register*, iv, 33.
15   *Aberdeen Council Register*, i, 395.
16   *Ibid*, ix, 90.
17   Milne, 27.
18   *Aberdeen Council Register*, lxiii, 119; lxv, 184.
19   Milne, 271.
20   *Aberdeen Council Register*, lxiii, 119; lxiv, 133.
21   Torrie, *Glasgow*, 43–57.
22   Fraser, *Street Names*, 87.
23   Milne, 272.
24   *Aberdeen Journal*, 30 June 1794; Fraser, *Street Names*, 88.
25   Duncan, 189.
26   Anderson, 68.
27   Stevenson, 'Trade with the south' in Lynch *et al*, 180; *Libellus de Vita et Miraculis Sancti Godrici*, 28–30; Brook, A J S, 'Technical Description of the Regalia of Scotland', *Proc Soc Antiq Scot*, xxiv (1889–90), 66 note 1.
28   *APS*, i, 11.
29   *RRS*, i, *no* 243.
30   *Ibid*, ii, *no* 153; *see* Duncan, 477–8, for a discussion of the meaning of the term *ansum* or hanse.
31   *Abdn Reg*, vol 1.
32   Wyness, 11.
33   *Ibid*, 11; Robertson, 26.
34   Murray, J C, 90, 246.
35   Murray, J C, 'The archaeological evidence' in Smith, *New Light*, 13.

36   Torrie, E P D 1992, 'The early urban site of New Aberdeen: a reappraisal of the evidence', *Northern Scotland*, xii, 1–18.
37   *See* **Aberdeen: the physical setting**.
38   Milne, 40–43.
39   *Ibid*, 35.
40   Gordon, *Map* **figure 6**.
41   MS *Burgh Sasine Register, Aberdeen*, i, 206; i, 414, for example.
42   *St Nich Cart*, i, 60.
43   Stones, *Friaries*, 38.
44   MS *Aberdeen City Archives*, press 19, bundle 24. Thanks are due to Miss J Cripps for her assistance.
45   MS *Aberdeen City Archives*, press 19, bundle 24.
46   MS *Aberdeen City Archives*, press 19, bundle 130, *nos* 130, 11 & 53.
47   MS *Aberdeen City Archives*, parcel N 6, description of plots lviii, lvi and lii; Colin Innes, *Plan of the Intended South Entry to Aberdeen 1798*.
48   Milne, 107.
49   *Ibid*, 106.
50   *Ibid*, 108.
51   *Ibid*, 109, 115.
52   Fraser, *Green*, 32.
53   Douglas, 84.
54   *St Nich Cart*, i, 107; i, 113; and ii, 95.
55   *Ibid*, i, 204 refers to two mills; *Abdn Recs*, i, 239.
56   *St Nich Cart*, i, 156. In 1533 the Council Register confirms of mills that there were 'two within the town and two without' (*Alphabetical Index to the First Volumes of the Council Register of the City of Aberdeen*, 417).
57   *Alphabetical Index to the First Volumes of the Council Register of the City of Aberdeen*, 421.
58   Milne, 41.
59   MS *Aberdeen City Archives*, box 33/17, 17/11, 17/12; also, viii, 72; viii, 271; viii, 451; viii, 522. Thanks are due to Dr Iain Fraser for the second set of references.
60   Milne, 33.
61   *Abdn Chrs*, i, 3.
62   Duncan, 482.
63   *Abdn Recs*, i, 21. Aberdeen University Library, MS M390, Mass 8/1; MS M390, Mass 15/1; MS M390, Mass 9/2.

28

64 *Abdn Recs*, i, li.
65 *Abdn Chrs*, viii, 12–14. Berwick had this status under Alexander III (1249–86), although no charter survives.
66 *Abdn Recs*, i, 82–90, 118–119.
67 *Abdn Chrs*, 4–5.
68 *Ibid*, iii, 5–8.
69 *Ibid*, 8–9.
70 *Ibid*, 290, 291.
71 The guild merchant claimed to control export trade in the staple goods of wool, woolfells and hides, and luxury items. This monopoly could not always be enforced. Alexander II's charter of 1122 confirmed the existence of the guild merchant in Aberdeen.
72 In 1326 Robert I granted the duties on red and white fish, which had pertained to the crown, to the burgesses of Aberdeen (Ewan, E, 'The Age of Bon-Accord', in Smith, *New Light*, 33).
73 Stevenson, A K W, 'Trade between Scotland and the Low Countries in the Later Middle Ages' (unpublished PhD thesis, University of Aberdeen, 1982), 20.
74 Murray, J C, 182.
75 *Ibid*, 197–200.
76 *Abdn Reg*, ii, 280.
77 Archaeological evidence, however, suggests that imported luxury goods were not of the same high quality and sophistication as those brought into Perth (Mr J C Murray, *pers comm*).
78 Ewan, E L, 'Burgesses of Fourteenth-Century Scotland' (unpublished PhD thesis, University of Edinburgh, 1984), 27; *MS Council Register*, vi 945; Booton, H, 'Sir John Rutherfurd: a Fifteenth-Century Aberdeen Burgess and Laird' in *Scottish Economic and Social History*, vol x (1990), 24.
79 Stones, *Two Burghs*, 12; *Abdn Recs*, i, 14.
80 *ER*, i, 61. The firing of the town may have been a result of Edward III's attack.
81 *Abdn Recs*, i, 105–106; Stones, J A in Murray, J C, 115.

82 Murray, J C, *passim*.
83 Booton, H, unpublished estimates.
84 *Abdn Recs*, i, 116, 174.
85 *Abdn Chrs*, viii.
86 *Abdn Recs*, i, 191.
87 *Ibid*, i, 91–92.
88 *APS*, i, 453b.
89 Keith, 59; Booton, H, unpublished calculations.
90 White, A, 'The Reformation in Aberdeen', in Smith, *New Light*, 63–5; White, A, 'The Impact of the Reformation on a Burgh Community: the Case of Aberdeen', in Lynch, M (ed), *The Early Modern Town in Scotland*, 81–101; *Abdn Recs*, i, 323–4.
91 *Abdn Recs*, i, 344; *Abdn Ecc Recs*, 3–12; White, A, 'The Regent Morton's Visitation: the Reformation of Aberdeen, 1574', in MacDonald, A A, Lynch, M & Cowan, I B (edd), *The Renaissance of Scotland*, 246–63.
92 *Aberdeen Description*, 5–6.
93 *Aberdeen Council Register*, i, 81.
94 *Ibid*, i, 422.
95 Mellor and Smith, 20 and information provided by Dr H Booton (unpublished); Booton, H, *pers comm*. Plague was technically not one but several diseases, bubonic plague being the most noted. The plague that hit much of the country in 1584–85 apparently had a minimal effect in Aberdeen, where ports were closed and access into the town curtailed in September 1584; the death penalty or permanent banishment was the punishment for harbouring strangers (who might have been infected) in May 1585 (*Aberdeen Council Register, 1570–1625*, ii, 52–54; ii, 57).
96 Henderson, 13; Smout, T C, 'Coping with plague in sixteenth- and seventeenth-century Scotland', *Scotia*, ii, *no* i, 23; Torrie, *Dunfermline*, xxiii–xxiv; *MS Council Records*, vii, 963; Booton, H, *pers comm*.
97 Wyness, 72.
98 Building work at York Place revealed disarticulated human remains,

probably plague victims buried in the sands, *Discovery and Excavation in Scotland*, 1987; Wyness, 73.

99 Mellor and Smith, 20.

100 *Aberdeen Description*, 9.

101 *Aberdeen Council Register*, i, 17.

102 Wyness, 65.

103 Fraser, *Historical Aberdeen*, 113.

104 Wyness, 65 and 64. Simpson and Stevenson give a full assessment of late medieval housing.

105 Booton, H, 'Inland trade: a study of Aberdeen in the later Middle Ages' in M Lynch *et al, The Scottish Medieval Town*,151.

106 *MS Aberdeen Council Register*, v 2, 722.60.

107 Booton, H, 'Inland trade', in Lynch *et al*, 153; *see also* Gibson, A J S and Smout, T C, *Prices, Food and Wages in Scotland*.

108 Lynch, M, 'Continuity and change in urban society, 1500–1700', in Houston, R A and Whyte, I D (edd), *Scottish Society, 1500–1800*, 116.

109 Booton, H, 'Inland trade', in Lynch *et al*, 153.

110 *Aberdeen Description*, 5.

111 Booton, H, 'Inland trade', in Lynch *et al*, 155.

112 Fraser, *Historic Aberdeen*, 32–33.

113 *Abdn Chrs*, 14.

114 Booton, H, 'Economic and social change in later medieval Aberdeen', in Smith, *New Light*, 47.

115 Brown, J J, 'The social, political and economic influences of the Edinburgh merchant elite, 1600–1638' (unpublished PhD thesis, University of Edinburgh, 1985), 112.

116 MacNiven, D, 'Merchants and traders in early seventeenth-century Aberdeen', in Stevenson, *Lairds to Louns*, 57.

117 Booton, H, 'Economic and social change in later medieval Aberdeen', in Smith, *New Light*,

50; Booton, H, 'The Craftsmen of Aberdeen between 1400 and 1550', *Northern Scotland*, xiii (1993), 4.

118 Lynch, 'Continuity and change', 96, 98; Lynch, 'Social and Economic Structure of the Larger Towns, 1450–1600', in Lynch *et al, The Scottish Medieval Town*, 269.

119 *MS Aberdeen Council Register*, vii, 623.

120 MacNiven, 'Merchants and traders in early seventeenth-century Aberdeen', in Stevenson, *Lairds to Louns*, 63.

121 Tyson, R E, 'The rise and fall of manufacturing in rural Aberdeenshire' in Smith, J S and Stevenson, D (edd), *Fermfolk and Fisherfolk*, 64–5.

122 For a discussion of this, *see* MacNiven, 'Merchants and traders in early seventeenth-century Aberdeen' in Stevenson (ed), *Lairds to Louns*; MacNiven, D, 'Merchants and traders in early seventeenth-century Aberdeen' (unpublished M Litt thesis, University of Aberdeen, 1977).

123 Devine, T M, 'The merchant class of the larger Scottish towns in the seventeenth and early eighteenth centuries', in Gordon, G and Dicks, B (edd), *Scottish Urban History*, 99, assesses the wealth of the merchant class in the 1690s. *See also* Torrie, 'The archaeological implications of development' in Torrie, *Glasgow*, 52–3.

124 Tyson, R E, 'Famine in Aberdeenshire, 1695–1699: anatomy of a crisis', in Stevenson, *From Lairds to Louns*, 32–52.

125 Tyson, R E, 'The population of Aberdeenshire, 1695–1755: a new approach', *Northern Scotland*, vi, *no* 2 (1985), 126–27.

126 On mills, *see also* **gazetteer**.

127 *See gazetteer*.

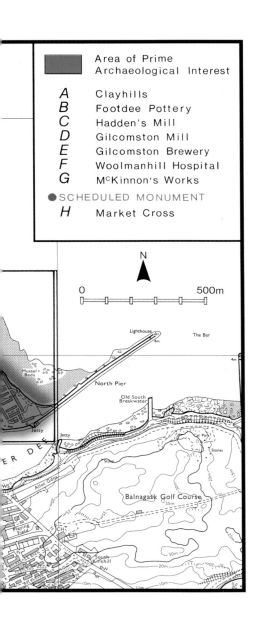

Area of Prime
Archaeological Interest

A   Clayhills
B   Footdee Pottery
C   Hadden's Mill
D   Gilcomston Mill
E   Gilcomston Brewery
F   Woolmanhill Hospital
G   McKinnon's Works

● SCHEDULED MONUMENT

H   Market Cross

N

0 ————————— 500m

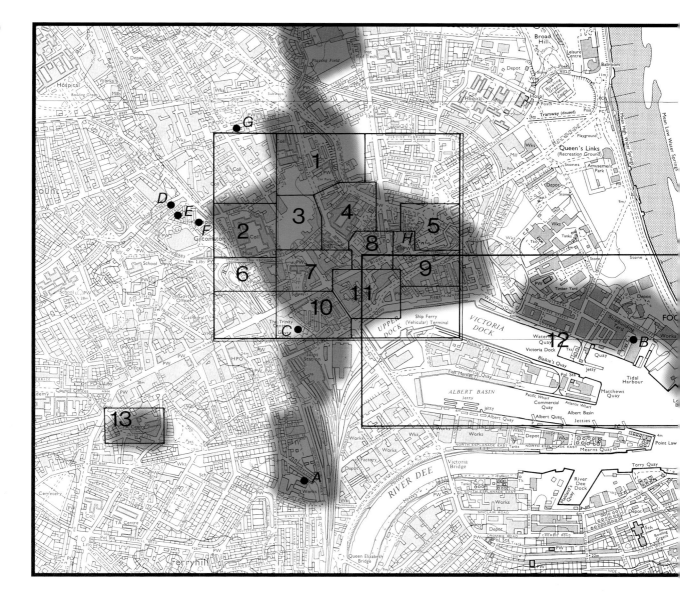

figure 8

The archaeological potential
of New Aberdeen

**the archaeology
of New Aberdeen**

Aberdeen has long been recognised as one of a small group of Scottish burghs which has preserved substantial archaeological levels despite large-scale nineteenth- and twentieth-century development. It is also unusual in that since 1976 it has had archaeologists in post (since 1979 as part of the Council establishment). There has therefore been a considerable amount of controlled excavation in the burgh of New Aberdeen over the last two decades, largely in response to city centre development hinging on oil-related prosperity. Aberdeen is also rare, in Scottish terms, in that it has a particularly well-preserved set of town records. Although not yet by any means adequately exploited, these can be used alongside the archaeological evidence to pinpoint those areas of the town where different types of urban activity took place. An additional asset is the map of the burgh by Parson James Gordon of Rothiemay **figure 6** which, although not accurate to modern cartographic standards, provides valuable information on the locations of the main features of the burgh, the town layout and its extent prior to subsequent urban development.

Excavation and archaeological recording work since 1973 have considerably added to the picture of the developing burgh from the twelfth century onwards. In all, some forty major excavations have taken place, their locations largely dictated by the exigencies of development, which has fortunately provided opportunities to test the nature and depth of archaeological deposits in many areas of the medieval burgh. The results from excavations are complemented by those from a large number of archaeological observations (watching briefs) on development works in progress. Evidence of medieval and later land use, property divisions and building types has been recovered from several areas of the town, and the recovery of large quantities of associated objects and environmental material has allowed the details of daily life, industrial activities and contacts beyond the burgh to be reconstructed. The survival and depth of the archaeological deposits in New Aberdeen is variable, although the paucity of remains in some areas has been more than compensated for by the wealth of surviving deposits in others. Where deposits have not been disturbed by later development, the survival of medieval levels with good quality organic, structural and artefactual remains is impressive. The tendency towards comparatively shallow deposits (typically, some 1.5 m of archaeological stratigraphy on a well-preserved medieval site) has meant that cellar-digging in the nineteenth century was particularly destructive. As a general rule, Victorian builders in the city tended to scarp the landscape extensively before construction, which has meant that post-medieval levels tend to survive less well than those of earlier date. Despite these counter-factors, however, Aberdeen has provided a massive resource of archaeological information on the development, growth and daily existence of an important historic Scottish burgh which is second to none—and which is still not fully exploited.

A number of key areas of the burgh had been developed before archaeological investigation became the norm. These include: the site of the castle, destroyed by the construction of a block of flats in the 1960s; the area around St Katherine's Hill, cut through by Union Street in the early 1800s; and much of the west side of Broad Street, occupied for the past twenty years by a major civic building, St Nicholas House. Confirmation of the absence of surviving archaeological deposits is an important aspect of the ongoing task of urban archaeological monitoring, for both pragmatic and research reasons. On the one hand, it allows better-informed archaeological responses to development proposals; and, on the other, it allows a picture to be built up of the extent of surviving archaeological deposits and features. For this reason, most of the archaeological watching briefs which have taken place are reported in the **area by area assessment** (*below*), even those which produced negative results. Today, a number of archaeologically sensitive areas still survive within the city centre and elsewhere; and there are several questions to which future investigations in appropriate locations may still provide answers. These areas are described in detail in the **area by area assessment** (*below*), but include the following major elements: the Justice Mills; the Shiprow and Harbour areas; the Franciscan Friary (its site now occupied by Marischal College); the sites of the ports; and some remaining frontages on Upperkirkgate, Schoolhill and Castlegate. In addition, the need to consider the wider context of the historic burgh has been recognised, and preliminary archaeological and historical studies of suburbs and hinterland are underway.

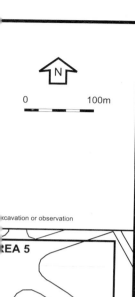

0   100m

xcavation or observation

REA 5

A 9

a Dock

area by area assessment

introduction

For this survey, the medieval core of New Aberdeen has been divided into twelve discrete areas *see* **figures 8** *&* **9**. The divisions into areas have been made arbitrarily and for the sake of convenience; they are not intended to reflect the development of the medieval or later burgh. The map for Area 12 **figure 37** also provides an area location map for the important harbour area. Areas 13 and 14 are not located in the cores of either Old or New Aberdeen but have been selected for detailed treatment because they contain features closely related to these two historic medieval burghs: Area 13 contains the site of the Justice Mills, and Area 14, the supposed location of the Leper Hospital.

area 1

Gallowgate: covering an area from Aberdeen College in the north-west, to West North Street in the north-east, to Mealmarket Street in the south-east, to the junction of Loch Street and Berry Street in the south-west **figure 10**

historic sites and monuments known from documentary and cartographic sources

Gallowgate Port

The Gallowgate Port (sometimes called Calsie or Causey Port) was the most northerly port controlling movement between New Aberdeen and Old Aberdeen and the north (*see also* pp 11–13 for information on the town's ports). By 1518, the Gallowgate Port was considered to be an ancient port and it was decorated with the royal arms.[1] At its demolition, sometime between 1769 and 1778,[2] its site had long been on Port Hill. It is possible, however, that in earlier medieval times the port may have been positioned further south and that it was gradually moved further north in response to town expansion—as may be witnessed in other towns.[3] No physical evidence for this port survives today and, to date, archaeological investigation has produced no direct evidence of this structure.

archaeological potential and future development

Parts of the Gallowgate area are of proven archaeological potential with excavations at *45–75 Gallowgate* (below) proving especially productive, both in terms of archaeological information and structures, and in terms of the rich artefactual and environmental evidence retrieved. In other areas, later disturbance may have removed most archaeological stratigraphy, although the work at *56 Gallowgate* demonstrated that medieval deposits could survive even beneath nineteenth-century cellars. Location of the Gallowgate Port would be particularly welcome. It is still a priority to ascertain the extent of the medieval loch and other waterlogged areas, since a better appreciation of the natural medieval environment and its limitations will help to elucidate the extent and growth of the early burgh.

No sites in Area 1 are known to be under threat from development at present. For the future, however, the few *frontage portions on Gallowgate* which have not been disturbed by recent development would particularly warrant archaeological investigation if opportunities arise. Other parts of Area 1 will clearly merit at least archaeological observation in the event of any ground disturbance.

previous archaeological work and chance finds

A *45–75 Gallowgate NJ 941 066 (see also* **area 3***)*

thirteenth- to twentieth-century evidence of backlands, fourteenth-century tannery
A substantial backland area within the defined Bon Accord Centre perimeter (a greatly

34

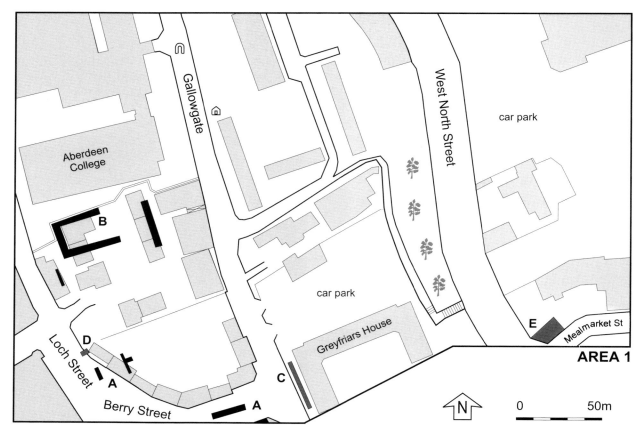

figure 10
Area 1
© Crown Copyright

figure 11

Late fourteenth-
century pottery
from the Gallowgate
excavation

Mar's Castle

A town house, known as Mar's Castle and thought to have been constructed in 1594,[4] stood at the top of Gallowgate and bore many similarities to its contemporary, Provost Ross' House (*see* **area 11**). It is believed to have been the residence of the Earls of Mar during the seventeenth century. It was demolished for road widening in 1897.

There are no historic standing buildings in Area 1 which fall within the scope of this survey.

notes

1	Milne, 271.
2	*MS Aberdeen City Archives*, lxiii, 119; lxiv, 133.
3	Torrie, *Glasgow*.
4	MacGibbon, D and Ross, T, v, 81–2; Bogdan, N Q and Bryce, I B D, 3.

history

archaeology

extended area to the north and west of 45–47 Gallowgate: *see* **area 3**) was excavated prior to re-development. This large-scale excavation recovered much useful information regarding the growth of the area between the loch and Gallowgate, in an archaeological sequence spanning the thirteenth to twentieth centuries **figure 11**.

The earliest use of this location seems to have been for gravel quarrying in the mid thirteenth century. In the later fourteenth century a tannery or skin yard was erected on the site, though this was dismantled by *c* 1400. Yard boundaries were established in the fifteenth and sixteenth centuries, perhaps marking the start of domestic building on the street frontages. Stone buildings were constructed in the mid seventeenth century and in the early eighteenth century an episcopal chapel was erected on the site.[6] Some evidence of the eastern edge of the loch was also recovered.

B *Loch Street, former City Taxis site NJ 940 067*

disturbed backland site
Trial trenches were excavated by machine to assess the archaeological potential of the site once occupied by the Ogston and Tennant Soap and Candle factory. The site was adjacent to areas where substantial medieval remains extending back from Gallowgate were recorded during previous excavations (45–75 Gallowgate: *see above*). On this present site, however, previous disturbance had removed any traces of the medieval backlands. Examination of natural levels adjacent to modern Loch Street indicated that the eastern edge of the medieval loch did not impinge upon the area of this site.[7]

C *56 Gallowgate NJ 941 066*

nineteenth-century cellars, possible medieval soil
The pavement in front of Greyfriars House, Gallowgate, was excavated to a depth of 1.5 m to provide a foundation for a new entrance and ramp. Archaeological observation showed the site to be within nineteenth-century cellars and to have been disturbed to a level just above the natural subsoil. A humic soil above natural, which may have been medieval in date, yielded bone but no dateable finds. The original east frontage of Gallowgate now lies beneath the street due to road widening earlier in the twentieth century.[8]

D *Loch Street service trench NJ 940 066*

medieval midden material
During the excavation of a service trench, animal bone and medieval pottery were removed from a midden layer *c* 2 m deep, located adjacent to the supposed edge of the medieval loch.[10]

E *56–58 West North Street NJ 943 066*

possible medieval marshland
Observation of construction trenches here showed no evidence of medieval features, but indicated that this area, low-lying in relation to the rising ground of Gallowgate, might have been marshland in the medieval period.

notes

6   Evans (forthcoming).
7   *Discovery and Excavation in Scotland*   9   *Discovery and Excavation in Scotland*
          1991.   1990.
8   Murray, J C, 110.

area 2

the northern part of the Denburn—covering an area from Woolmanhill in the north-west, to the junction of George Street and Loch Street in the north-east, to Schoolhill in the south-east, to His Majesty's Theatre in the south-west **figure 12**

historic sites and monuments known from documentary and cartographic sources

Dominican Friary

The Dominican Friary (a house of the Dominican or Black Friars) is said to have been founded in Aberdeen by Alexander II sometime between 1222[1] and 1249.[2] There is some evidence that it was in existence by 1257[3] and from the fourteenth century it features regularly in documentary sources.[4] The friary was situated on the outskirts of urban settlement on the later-named Schoolhill at a site now occupied by part of Robert Gordon's College, the Robert Gordon University, and Aberdeen Art Gallery. There are few details of the layout of the friary, but newspaper articles detailing the finds made during building operations on the site between 1833 and 1923 appear to indicate that the main complex and church were situated at the present college gymnasium.[5] As well as the church and the usual residential and domestic buildings, which presumably existed, there was a barn, a kiln, a dovecot and a garden and orchard.[6] By 1503, the complex housed a prior and thirteen

---

archaeological potential and future development

Much of the archaeology of this important area seems to have been removed by comprehensive scarping in the nineteenth century. Any future developments in or around the site of the *Dominican Friary*, however, will require very careful archaeological observation, including any episodes of ground disturbance within and around parts of *Robert Gordon's College*, the *Robert Gordon University*, and *Aberdeen Art Gallery*. Even in scarped areas, the potential for the survival of fragmentary or isolated features should be recognised, as evidenced by the wall foundation at *2–16 Harriet Street*. No sites in Area 2 are known to be under threat from development at present.

previous archaeological work and chance finds

A *2–16 Harriet Street* NJ *963 065*

fourteenth- to fifteenth-century wall
This area, adjacent to the site of the medieval Dominican Friary, founded in the late thirteenth century, had been comprehensively scarped in the nineteenth century. One feature was observed, however, a stone wall foundation which may have dated to the fourteenth or fifteenth century.[18]

B *28 Harriet Street* NJ *939 064*

no archaeological results
Observation during building work indicated an absence of archaeological deposits overlying natural subsoil levels.[19]

C *Rear of Aberdeen Art Gallery, Blackfriars Street* NJ *938 063*

no archaeological results
Observation of this small area, adjacent to the site of the medieval Dominican Friary, produced no pre-modern levels.[20]

friars.[7] The house was destroyed by the Protestant reformers in 1560,[8] and its pertinents passed to George, Earl Marischal in 1587[9] who endowed them on the new Marischal College.[10]

Excavation and observation during building works has so far produced no direct evidence of the friary (*see* 2–16 Harriet Street; 28 Harriet Street; and Rear of Aberdeen Art Gallery, below), but, given the historical importance of the friary, archaeological monitoring of any future works in this vicinity is strongly recommended.

Grammar School

A school was founded in Aberdeen by at least the thirteenth century. In 1262 one Thomas de Benholm is referred to as rector of the school of Aberdeen;[11] but the first specific mention of a grammar school is not until 1418 when John Homyll was appointed as rector to replace Andrew de Scheveze, deceased.[12]

The medieval grammar school had close ties with the church, although by as early as 1479 the council was collecting funds to pay the master of the grammar school £6 per annum.[13] The school was situated near the Dominican House and St Nicholas Church on Schoolhill. Historical research has not yet revealed details of the structure, but the medieval grammar school would not have been a large institution, probably no larger than one or two rooms. By 1527 the building was 'decaden and abill to fall down',[14] and the town council ordered its repair. Two years later the town further assisted the grammar school and its master by voting £10 Scots to supplement his board, because the school was 'desert and destitute of barnis'.[15] The town accounts show on-going repairs to the school particularly to the roof which was thatched.[16] In 1624 the school was replaced with a new building, which housed scholars until 1757, when it, too, was replaced by another sited in the grounds of the former Dominican Friary. To date no archaeological evidence of the grammar school has been found.

Robert Gordon's College

A further educational establishment was founded in 1730, Robert Gordon's College, for the maintenance of boys 'whose parents were in indigent circumstances'.[17]

There are no historic standing buildings in Area 2 which fall within the scope of this survey.

notes

history

1	Robertson, 26.	4	*ER*, i, 60 onwards.
2	*Aberdeen Friars*, 11.	5	Stones, *Two Burghs*, 18.
3	Cowan and Easson, 116.	6	*Aberdeen Friars*, 108.

archaeology

D *Extension to Robert Gordon's College NJ 938 065*

no archaeological results
Observation during construction of the extension produced no evidence of archaeological levels above the subsoil.[21]

E *Robert Gordon's College NJ 938 065*

probable eighteenth-century well
A well, probably dating to the eighteenth century, was recorded below the floor of a classroom in the college.[22]

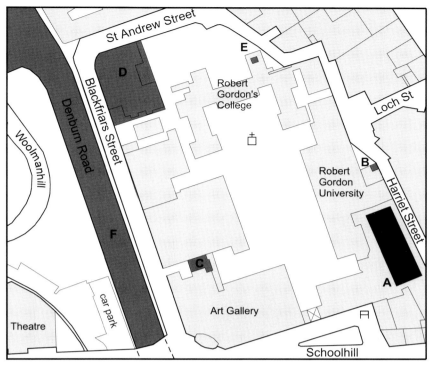

AREA 2

A   2 - 16 Harriet Street
B   28 Harriet Street
C   rear of Aberdeen Art Gallery
D   extension to Robert Gordon's College
E   Robert Gordon's College, well
F   Denburn Road construction

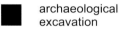 site of Dominican Friary

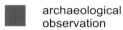 site of Grammar School

N   0   50m

◼ archaeological excavation

◾ archaeological observation

figure 12

Area 2

© Crown Copyright

history

7   Cowan and Easson, 116.
8   *Aberdeen Friars*, 97.
9   *Ibid*, 108.
10   *Ibid*, 112.
11   Keith, 104.
12   *Aberdeen Council Register*, i, 37.

13   Wyness, 46.
14   *Aberdeen Council Register*, i, 120.
15   *Ibid*, i, 122.
16   *Ibid*, i, 120; *Accounts, Extracts*, 118.
17   *See also* Fraser, *Thesis*.

archaeology

F *Denburn road construction NJ 939 061–937 064 (see also* **area 6***)*

no archaeological results
Observation during road building did not indicate the presence of archaeological deposits.[23]
notes

18   Murray, J C, 96–99.
19   *Ibid*, 108.
20   *Ibid*, 107–108.
21–3 Further information from Arts and

Recreation Department, Arts
and Museums, Art Gallery,
Schoolhill, Aberdeen, AB10 1FQ.

area 3

area now covered by the Bon Accord shopping centre, also the lower end of Schoolhill, and Upperkirkgate at the south, and the junction of Loch Street and George Street to the north **figure 13**

historic sites and monuments known from documentary and cartographic sources

Upperkirkgate Port or Schoolhill Port

The Upperkirkgate port or Schoolhill Port stood on Schoolhill, just within the mill burn (*see* pp 11–13 for further information on the town's ports). It was probably in existence by the fifteenth century. By the time of its demolition in 1794, a gallery or room had been constructed above it, which was perhaps erected as early as 1585.[1] The port and gallery were purchased by the town council in 1793 for £140,[2] and demolished a year later.[3] To date there is no archaeological evidence of this structure.

George Jamesone's House, Schoolhill

This late sixteenth-century house was used by George Jamesone (1588–1644) as a studio on Schoolhill, on his return from studying art in Antwerp. This tall turreted house **figure 14** was demolished in the 1880s to be replaced by a row of tenements. To date there is no archaeological evidence of this structure.

archaeological potential and future development

The excavations at *45–47 Gallowgate* and at *45–75 Gallowgate* were very rich, both in terms of the structures revealed and the artefacts and environmental evidence recovered. In addition, the excavations produced well-stratified sequences of occupation phases and other activities spanning some 700 years. Stratified sites of this type are of great importance to urban archaeology and yield by far the most information. Several other sites in Area 3 were hardly any less rich, with that at *42 St Paul Street* yielding much important information on the early buildings of the burgh and the evolution of property divisions. Comparison of the 42 St Paul Street findings with those from the *30–46 Upperkirkgate* site, where important archaeological deposits and some special finds also survived, may suggest that the medieval settlement gradually developed downhill from Broad Street. As well as well-stratified sites, midden deposits can be useful sources of archaeological information: these, too, have been found in Area 3, observed in the *British Telecom trenches*. The area has also produced a medieval *coin hoard* which is a reminder of the potential for important chance discoveries. Clearly, this area has very high archaeological potential.

No sites in Area 3 are known to be under threat from development at present but, given the relative wealth of surviving evidence which has been recovered thus far (*see below*), rigorous archaeological monitoring of development proposals must continue, and arrangements for excavation must be made wherever appropriate. In particular, any development which disturbs the ground along the *north frontage of Upperkirkgate* should certainly be subject to archaeological investigation. The recovery of any evidence for the *Upperkirkgate Port* or of any *town defences* would also be a high priority.

previous archaeological work and chance finds

A *45–47 Gallowgate NJ 941 065*

twelfth- to nineteenth-century occupation, sill-beam and wattle building evidence
Excavation in a pend opening on to Gallowgate yielded a succession of fifteen occupation phases dating from the late twelfth to the nineteenth century, with stratified deposits

figure 13
Area 3
© Crown Copyright

	archaeological excavation
	archaeological observation

A   45 - 47 Gallowgate
B   45 - 75 Gallowgate
C   42 St Paul Street
D   30 - 46 Upperkirkgate
E   43 - 57 Upperkirkgate
F   42 Loch Street
G   Donald's Court, 16 Schoolhill
H   42 Upperkirkgate
I   Upperkirkgate coin hoard
J   British Telecom trench

⋂   site of Upperkirkgate Port
⌂   site of George Jamesone's House
◎   site of coin hoard

AREA 3

figure 14
George Jamesone's
House, Schoolhill

42

figure 15

Late thirteenth- or
early fourteenth-
century pit,
with remains of
wattle cover, from the
42 St Paul Street
excavation
© Crown Copyright,
Historic Scotland

figure 16

Foundations of
a thirteenth- to
fourteenth-century
post-and-wattle
building, from the
42 St Paul Street
excavation
© Crown Copyright,
Historic Scotland

water supply

The mill dam, or burn, passed over Upperkirkgate near the port, but whether to the east or west is not clear from secondary or cartographic source material, most of which is unreliable on this point[4] (*see* pp 15–17 for further information on the town's water supplies).

town defences

history

There is some indication from cartographic sources for the presence of town defences in this area (*see* pp 11–13 for further information on town defences). Parson Gordon's map of

archaeology

reaching *c* 2.5 m deep. A period of dumping in the late twelfth or thirteenth century was followed, as Gallowgate developed, by the construction of a building with a grooved sill-beam on a stone foundation. This had been destroyed by a ditch which was replaced by a wattle-lined drain, both near to the boundary, which was continued throughout the fourteenth century by a series of wattle fences. Later in the fourteenth century, two sill-beam structures were successively built on the site and a floor and wattle wall may have been part of a building or yard, all respecting this boundary. Only fragments of the buildings were in the excavated area; the rest had been cut away by the later cellars. In the fifteenth and sixteenth centuries a pend was established on the boundary, with three superimposed paths, the uppermost made of well-set cobbles. This appeared to have become an internal passageway in the nineteenth-century building which was demolished several years prior to excavation.[6]

B *45–75 Gallowgate NJ 941 066 (see also* **area 1***)*

thirteenth- to twentieth-century evidence, fourteenth-century tannery
A substantial backland area within the defined Bon Accord Centre perimeter (a greatly extended area to the north and west of 45–47 Gallowgate) was excavated prior to re-development. This large-scale excavation recovered much useful information regarding the growth of the area between the loch and Gallowgate, in an archaeological sequence spanning the thirteenth to twentieth centuries **figure 11**.

   The earliest use of this location seems to have been for gravel quarrying in the mid thirteenth century. In the later fourteenth century a tannery or skin yard was erected on the site, though this was dismantled by *c* 1400. Yard boundaries were established in the fifteenth and sixteenth centuries, perhaps marking the start of domestic building on the street frontages. Stone buildings were constructed in the mid seventeenth century and in the early eighteenth century an episcopal chapel was erected on the site.[7] Some evidence of the eastern edge of the loch was also recovered.

C *42 St Paul Street NJ 941 065*

thirteenth- to fourteenth-century buildings, property boundaries, oven, pits
Archaeological and historical investigation at this site has provided a fairly full picture of the changes in the layout of this backland area adjacent to Upperkirkgate from the early thirteenth century until the present day. Properties were laid out from *c* 1200, at right angles to Upperkirkgate. Initially properties were of unequal size, but at the beginning of the fourteenth century the boundaries were re-organised to create more regular rigs. Some amalgamation later took place, when a large stone building was constructed on two adjacent properties some time in the fifteenth- to seventeenth-century period. In general terms, however, boundaries seem not to have changed after the mid fifteenth century when historical records of this site begin. Portions of a number of backlands buildings of post-and-wattle construction **figure 16** were also recovered, along with a bread oven and a large number of pits **figure 15**, which may have included storage among their original uses, in addition to cess-pit and rubbish disposal functions.[8]

1661 **figure 6** indicates what may have been a bank along the line of Upperkirkgate Port, Netherkirkgate Port and the loch, which may have been a man-made defence along the edge of the town not protected by natural features.[5] Excavations at 43–57 Upperkirkgate, however, offered no supporting archaeological evidence (*see below*).

There are no historic standing buildings in Area 3 which fall within the scope of this survey.

notes

1   Fraser, *Street Names*, 87.
2   Milne, 272.
3   *Aberdeen Journal*, 30 June 1794; Fraser, *Street Names*, 88.
4   *MS Aberdeen Archives*, box 33/17, 17/11, 17/12; *MS Council Records*, viii,

72; viii, 271; viii, 451; viii, 522. Thanks are due to Dr Iain Fraser for the second set of references.
5   Murray, J C, 246–7.

history

archaeology

D *30–46 Upperkirkgate NJ 941 064*

medieval and post-medieval occupation
A total area of 1,500 sq m was examined, encompassing a large backland site up to 10 m from the Upperkirkgate frontage, which was itself inaccessible because of the presence of standing buildings. The site lay *c* 6 m west of the area excavated at *no* 42 St Paul Street (*see above*). Much of the late medieval/early post-medieval deposits had been scarped during nineteenth-century development, but sufficient remained to allow some archaeological interpretation of the area to be made. It may be that this site was not developed so early or so intensively as 42 St Paul Street, perhaps suggesting that settlement developed gradually downhill from the Broad Street—Castle Street centre of the burgh. A clay foundation aligned north to south probably represented the remains of a thirteenth- to fourteenth-century boundary. No other early boundaries were recorded but most were probably on the lines of modern property divisions and have long since disappeared. The basal portions of a number of wooden posts were discovered, which may have represented the remnants of a medieval building near the frontage, but all other evidence of it had been obliterated. A number of medieval pits, of which three were very straight-sided and regular in shape, may have originally been storage pits. A thirteenth- to fourteenth-century pit had been lined with thin strips of timber. Medieval finds included a bone knife handle, two pieces of carved wood (perhaps from a casket), and a copper alloy enamelled brooch.[9]

E *43–57 Upperkirkgate NJ 941 063 (see also* **area 7***)*

fifteenth- to sixteenth-century buildings
This site on the south side of Upperkirkgate produced evidence of thirteenth- to twentieth-century activity. Cellarage and road widening had destroyed any traces of street frontage deposits, but remains of some fifteenth- to sixteenth-century buildings had survived. No evidence was found of the Upper Mill (*see* **area 7**), nor of the possible 'defensive bank' visible on Parson Gordon's map of 1661 (*see above*).

F *42 Loch Street, 14–21 Drum's Lane NJ 940 065*

boundary ditch, Edward 1 pennies
This area was examined following the discovery by demolition workers of two sterlings of Edward 1, and in an attempt to establish how far medieval activity extended northwards towards the Loch of Aberdeen. The site lay to the north of that later excavated at 30–46

Upperkirkgate (*see* above).[10] A simple sequence of post-medieval and medieval garden soil over the natural subsoil was established; a cess-pit and a possible east to west aligned boundary ditch were discovered cut into the subsoil.[11]

G *Donald's Court, 16 Schoolhill NJ 940 063*

no archaeological results
A small trial pit, excavated here prior to alterations, revealed natural gravel subsoil beneath the car-park surface in the court.[12]

H *42 Upperkirkgate NJ 941 064*

medieval pit
The dangerous condition and subsequent demolition of this listed frontage afforded a rare opportunity to examine a frontage site on Upperkirkgate. Natural subsoil, almost directly below floor level, was overlain by a thin layer (*c* 3 to 5 cm in depth) of medieval occupation. A pit, located near the street front, *c* 1 m in diameter and 1 m deep, had some 5 cm of thick red clay lining in its base. A small amount of thirteenth- to fourteenth-century pottery was recovered.

I *Ross's Court, Upperkirkgate c NJ 941 064*

fourteenth-century coin hoard
This discovery of more than 12,000 coins in 1886 is one of the largest to have been found anywhere in Britain, and is thought to have been deposited in the ground after 1331–5. As with the other hoards found in Aberdeen city centre (*see also* **areas 4** *&* **7**), more than 90 per cent of its contents consisted of English silver pennies, the remainder comprising pennies of Scotland, Ireland and the Continent. The hoard was found in a large bronze cauldron **figure 26**, which was probably a locally-made example of a style common throughout north-west Europe. (For details of other coin hoards found in Aberdeen, *see* **gazetteer**.)

J *British Telecom trenches NJ 940 064, NJ 941 065, NJ 942 065 (see also* **area 4***)*

medieval organic deposits near eastern edge of burgh
The insertion of a series of service trenches was observed archaeologically during the laying of a new major telephone cable along St Paul Street, Loch Street, Gallowgate, Upperkirkgate and Littlejohn Street. Thick organic medieval deposits were observed in Gallowgate, Upperkirkgate and the east end of St Paul Street. There was little medieval evidence from the west end of St Paul Street or from Loch Street.

In Littlejohn Street there were thick organic midden layers at the west end, from the top of the hill to approximately halfway down the hill where they ceased abruptly. This confirms the estimated extent of the medieval town in this direction. There was no surviving evidence of a ditch or any boundary, but it is unlikely that a fence would have been identifiable in the very narrow trenches. The trenches cutting across Gallowgate and Littlejohn Street road surfaces revealed no evidence of earlier street surfaces as the ground had previously been disturbed by the insertion of existing service trenches. All the medieval layers yielded a quantity of medieval pottery, leather, slag and bone.[13]

notes

6	Murray, H K, 303–13. *See also* Murray, J C, 114.	9	Cameron and Stones (forthcoming).
7	Evans (forthcoming).	10	*Ibid.*
8	*Discovery and Excavation in Scotland* 1986, 13.	11	Murray, J C, 109–110.
		12	*Ibid*, 109.
		13	*Ibid*, 110–112.

area 4
Gallowgate to the north-west, West North Street to the north-east and Broad Street to the south-west
figure 17

historic sites and monuments known from documentary and cartographic sources

Franciscan friary

Members of the Observant or Franciscan Friars, commonly called Greyfriars, may have been working in Aberdeen from 1461.[1] Their house was erected around 1469 as a result of endowments and land from Richard Vaus, burgh officials and others.[2] The friary was at the east side of Broad Street on the site of the present Marischal College; this was in the heart of the settlement which was an unusual situation for a friary. The location was, in all probability, determined by the availability of waste tenements owned by Vaus, since archaeological evidence suggests that the east side of Broad Street was in decline in the fourteenth century, a process that was to accelerate in the fifteenth. No documentary evidence has come to light on the friary complex and its first church, but in 1518–32 a new larger church was built for the friars by Bishop Gavin Dunbar **figure 18**.[3]

It has been estimated that the group consisted of twelve to sixteen friars.[4] In December 1559 the friars resigned all their possessions to the town council, thereby avoiding destruction of their property, and the council determined to maintain the house for the use of the town.[5] In 1567, some of the property of the Greyfriars was designated for conversion into a hospital[6] and in 1593 certain remaining buildings passed to George Keith, Earl Marischal, who endowed them on Marischal College.[7]

Greyfriars Church

The church was not quite conventionally aligned east to west, probably because of its position at the end of the building site. By the eighteenth century it was shortened by one bay to the north to permit easier access to Marischal College and extended at the east. Otherwise, it survived largely intact until 1903 when it was removed to make way for a new frontage to the college. The fine south window was, however, rebuilt into the east gable of

---

archaeological potential and future development

It would be useful to test the hypothesis that there was a *market* site in Broadgate which was later colonised by buildings—if opportunities arise for future archaeological investigation in this area.

The north-eastern part of Area 4, near Gallowgate, as with all the sites on or near Gallowgate in Area 3, has high archaeological potential. In Area 4, this was demonstrated on the *Gallowgate Middle School* site, with its exciting discovery of an early pit filled with leather and other organic materials. As in Area 3, the find of yet another *coin hoard* is a reminder of the potential discovery of significant chance finds in the city centre.

The church and conventual buildings of the *Franciscan Friary* now lie beneath the nineteenth- and twentieth-century structures of Marischal College (University of Aberdeen). Although the plan of the church is known in its latest phase, its earlier development is unrecorded, as is the nature of any conventual buildings.[15] Any further development in the area should be closely monitored. It should always be remembered that historic standing buildings, such as *Provost Skene's House*, may preserve archaeological evidence both within and beneath their structures, as well as within their grounds. Current proposals to convert part of Marischal College into an hotel will require archaeological evaluation of a portion of the Franciscan friary site. No other sites in this area are presently known to be under threat from development.

47

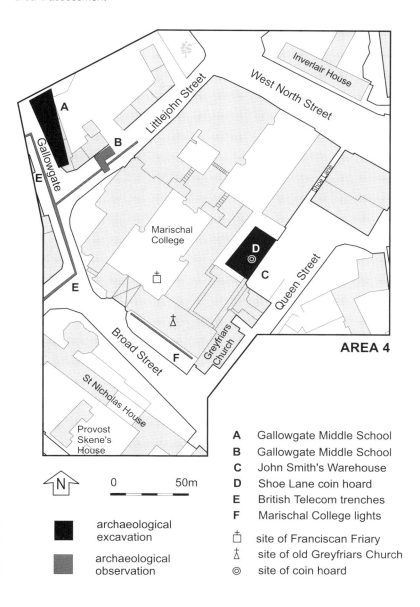

A	Gallowgate Middle School
B	Gallowgate Middle School
C	John Smith's Warehouse
D	Shoe Lane coin hoard
E	British Telecom trenches
F	Marischal College lights

⌂ site of Franciscan Friary
⊼ site of old Greyfriars Church
◎ site of coin hoard

■ archaeological excavation

▨ archaeological observation

figure 17
Area 4
© Crown Copyright,
Historic Scotland

figure 18
Old Greyfriars
Church, demolished
in 1903

48

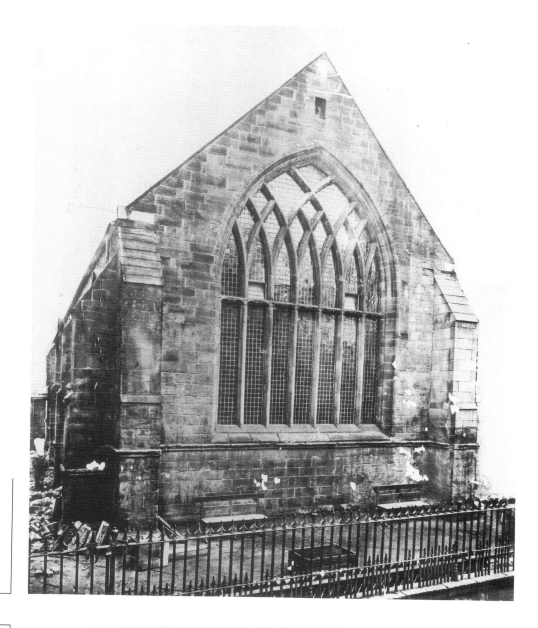

figure 19
Window in the
old Greyfriars
Church, later
reconstructed in
the new Greyfriars
Church

figure 20
Provost Skene's
House, Guest Row

the new Greyfriars Church **figure 19**. To date there is no direct archaeological evidence of the friary (*but see* John Smith's Warehouse, Queen Street; and Shoe Lane coin hoard, below).

burgh market

It has been mooted that a market may have existed in Broadgate (modern Broad Street), and that the island blocks of 6-67 Broad Street between Guest Row and Broad Street may represent later colonisation of the original wide market area.[8] The statement of Gordon that Guest Row and Broadgate were originally one street is used to support this theory.[9] There is, however, documentary evidence that Guest Row was an established street by 1439 at the latest, and continued in existence.[10] This enlarged area did not in consequence function as a second market in the fifteenth century and the hypothesis that it was the site of an early market has yet to be proved historically or archaeologically— although this latter view may perhaps be supported by findings of large amounts of butchered bone at Broad Street and filletted fish bone at Gallowgate.[11] If the first urban settlement was in the Green area, the early market place would have been at the east end of the Green (pp 14–15; *see also* Area 10). Cartographic evidence might support this theory, as a block of triangular development on Gordon's map **figure 6** might suggest market repletion.[12] (*See* p 19 for further background on the siting of the market.)

water supply

It has been suggested that in the early Middle Ages a water supply was diverted down the east side of Guest Row, before houses had been built, to run a mill (the Upper Mill) at the foot of Broad Street and Guest Row. So far, however, there is no archaeological or documentary evidence to support this theory.

historic standing buildings

Marischal College

In 1593, George Keith, Earl Marischal, founded the University of Marischal College, perhaps in reaction to lack of change in King's College, Old Aberdeen, and in order to operate a new reformed syllabus at New Aberdeen. The college was endowed with revenues from the Dominican and Carmelite properties, and was housed in the former Franciscan Friary on the east side of Broad Street. The buildings were altered on several occasions until 1836-44 when old buildings were removed to form the eastern side of the present quadrangle, designed by Archibald Simpson. The existing west side was constructed between 1893 and 1906, to designs by A Marshall Mackenzie, and necessitated the removal of the old Greyfriars Church (*see above*). The rebuilding provided a new examination hall, as well as an extension to the central tower. The work left Marischal College the second largest granite building in the world (after the Escorial in Madrid), and the granite was used in ways that previously had not been thought possible.[13] The Marischal College remained an independent university until 1860, when it united with King's College, Old Aberdeen.

Provost Skene's House, Guest Row

This outstanding piece of domestic architecture is one of the few remaining early buildings in the town **figure 20**. The earliest section is a three-storey wing perhaps dating from the mid sixteenth century. The interior has a painted gallery of 1626, which contains an important cycle of religious paintings; and some other seventeenth-century additions remain intact, for example a fine ceiling in one of the bedrooms. The house was owned by Sir George Skene, provost of Aberdeen in 1676–1685; used by the Duke of Cumberland in February 1746 on route north to crush the Jacobites; and was restored in the twentieth century.[14]

history

archaeology

notes

1 Cowan and Easson, 130.
2 Bryce, i, 307.
3 *Ibid*, 314–16.
4 *Ibid*, 318.
5 *Aberdeen Friars*, 97.
6 *Ibid*, 100.
7 Cowan and Easson, 130.
8 Murray, J C, 246. Guest Row, which once ran parallel to Broad Street on its west side, was largely obliterated by the construction of St Nicholas House. A remnant of it can be seen in Area 7. *See also* conjectural sketch map **figure 5**.
9 *Aberdeen Description*, 11.
10 *Abdn Reg*, i, 239.
11 Thanks are due to Mr J C Murray for this information.
12 *See* Gordon, **cartographic sources**.
13 Brogden, 24–26; *see also* Smith, *A Visitor's Guide to Marischal College*.
14 Brogden, 23–24.
15 Cameron, *Gallowgate* (forthcoming); for previous work on this area *see* notes 4 & 5.

previous archaeological work and chance finds

A & **B** *Gallowgate Middle School, Gallowgate NJ 941 065*

twelfth- to thirteenth-century pit, leather and environmental remains
This site was considered to have archaeological potential because of its location near the medieval street frontage, although the east side of Gallowgate had been moved back earlier in the twentieth century, sealing the previous line below the pavement and thoroughfare. In the event, there was found to have been considerable disturbance by nineteenth-century tenement foundations and the swimming pool of the Middle School. However, a large late twelfth- to early thirteenth-century pit was excavated, containing over fifty leather boots and shoes, belt fragments, leather trimmings, antler offcuts, a wooden scutching knife (for flax-working), a piece of moss rope and other environmental remains **figure 21**. This site, with its rare survival of impressive organic evidence including waste organic materials from various craft industries, helps to set previous work in the Gallowgate area in context.[16]

figure 21
Objects from the twelfth- to thirteenth-century pit, Gallowgate Middle School

C *John Smith's Warehouse, Queen Street NJ 943 064*

early medieval dumping, Franciscan Friary precinct, coin hoard
A machine trench was dug and development observed over the area of a demolished
warehouse to the rear of Broad Street. There was a substantial amount of garden soil
containing a small quantity of medieval pottery. Immediately over the natural subsoil was
a layer with heavily compacted organic remains. This seems consistent with an area
which, in the later 15th and 16th centuries may have been within the confines of the
Franciscan Friary, and in the earlier medieval period was probably used for dumping,
lying as it did at least 100m back from the Broad Street frontage.[17] In May 1847, the Shoe
Lane coin hoard was found on this site (*see below*).

D *Shoe Lane NJ 943 064*

sixteenth-century coin hoard
While digging foundations at Shoe Lane for an extension to John Smith's premises in May
1847 (*see* John Smith's Warehouse, Queen Street, above),[18] a very sizeable coin hoard of
low denomination coinage was found, comprising lions or hardheads of Mary Queen of
Scots dated between 1558 and 1560. It had been deposited in the ground in three bags,
one of canvas and two of leather, and though only a few coins now survive (in the
collections of Marischal Museum), the hoard was reported at the time of its discovery to
weigh about two hundredweight. If the hoard had any connection with the Franciscan
Friary, as is at least possible, then it would have represented a very large share of their
fortunes—almost the equivalent of five years' income of their wealthiest rivals in
Aberdeen. Evidence recovered during recent archaeological observation confirmed that
the coins are likely to have been deposited in open ground, either within the friary
precincts or on an adjacent backland area.[19]

E *British Telecom trenches NJ 940 064, NJ 941 065, NJ 942 065 (see also* **area 3***)*

medieval organic deposits near eastern edge of burgh
The insertion of a series of service trenches was archaeologically observed during the
laying of a new major telephone cable along St Paul Street, Loch Street, Gallowgate,
Upperkirkgate and Littlejohn Street. Thick organic medieval deposits were observed in
Gallowgate, Upperkirkgate and the east end of St Paul Street. There was little medieval
evidence from the west end of St Paul Street or from Loch Street.
   In Littlejohn Street there were thick organic midden layers at the west end, from the
top of the hill to approximately halfway down the hill where they ceased abruptly. This

confirms the estimated extent of the medieval town in this direction. There was no surviving evidence of a ditch or any boundary, but it is unlikely that a fence would have been identifiable in the very narrow trenches. The trenches cutting across Gallowgate and Littlejohn Street road surfaces revealed no evidence of earlier street surfaces as the ground had previously been disturbed by the insertion of existing service trenches. All the medieval layers yielded a quantity of medieval pottery, leather, slag and bone.[20]

F *Marischal College lights NJ 942 064*

garden soil and modern rubble
The excavation of narrow trenches for the installation of floodlighting along the west frontage of the College was observed archaeologically.[21] Garden soil and some probably early twentieth-century building rubble were noted.

notes

16   Cameron, *Warehouse*, 13.
17   Evans and Thain, 331–2.
18   Cameron, *Warehouse*, 13.
19   Murray, J C, 110–112.
20   Cooper, 71–87.

21   Further information from Arts and Recreation Department, Arts and Museums, Art Gallery, Schoolhill, Aberdeen, AB10 1FQ.

area 5

East North Street, Commerce Street, and Justice Street **figure 22**

historic sites and monuments known from documentary and cartographic sources

the castle

A castle was in existence in Aberdeen by 1264 at latest. The Exchequer Rolls for this year detail expenses incurred in its provisioning. Payment was also made for building work on the castle, although this was probably of the nature of repair or extension rather than the commencement of the construction of the castle since it already by this date housed a chapel.[1] It is presumed that the fortification was placed on the later-named Castle Hill, although the primary source material does not state its exact site. It is possible that some form of castle had existed in Aberdeen from the first founding of the burgh, although Castle Hill was no more favoured a situation than St Katherine's Hill since neither offered a ready water supply.[2] A highly speculative theory is that an earlier castle or fortification

archaeological potential and future development

No excavations have been carried out in Area 5 to date. Despite the consequent lack of evidence so far for archaeological traces either of the castle or St Ninian's Chapel, both of these features are highly significant for the early history of the burgh and, therefore, any ground disturbance, of whatever scale, particularly in the area of the castle, must be very carefully observed archaeologically. No development proposals are currently envisaged for this area.

figure 22
Area 5
© Crown Copyright

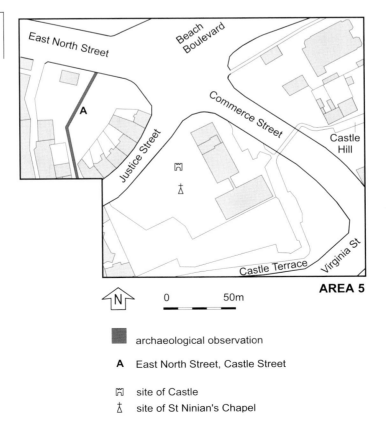

AREA 5

N   0   50m

◼ archaeological observation

A East North Street, Castle Street

⌂ site of Castle
⚐ site of St Ninian's Chapel

had been positioned on St Katherine's Hill. If this was indeed the case, the clustering of the first dwellings at the base of St Katherine's Hill, rather than Castle Hill, for protection, could partially explain the early development of the town in this area, rather than at the eastern end of Castlegate. Sometime during the early fourteenth century the castle appears to have been destroyed, most probably during the Wars of Independence. Lack of water would make the Castle Hill highly susceptible to successful siege. It was still standing in July 1308, however, after the supposed occasion of the razing of the castle to the ground by the burgesses of Aberdeen with their rallying cry of 'Bon Accord'. On 10 July Edward II instructed his admiral William le Betour to gather reinforcements from Hartlepool, Newcastle, Berwick on Tweed and other strongholds to assist in raising the siege of Aberdeen Castle.[3] Documentary evidence for the castle after this event has so far not come to light. The office of warden, however, remained hereditary in the family of Kennedy of Carmuc, who retained the title of Constable of Aberdeen until the end of the sixteenth century.[4]

Archaeological investigations have so far produced no direct evidence of the castle, though excavations in Virginia Street and to the south of Castlegate (*see* **area 9** *&* **11**) have produced evidence of medieval deposits in its probable vicinity.

St Ninian's Chapel, Castle Hill

There was a chapel housed in the castle by 1264 at latest. After the destruction of the castle sometime in the early fourteenth century, according to some secondary sources, a chapel dedicated to St Ninian was placed on Castle Hill as successor to the Castle Chapel. It has, however, also been argued that the chapel was not founded until 1504, when it was *noviter constructe super montem castri*.[5] This was still standing in 1661, although it ceased to function purely as a place of worship after the Reformation. In 1566, the east end of the chapel was converted into a lighthouse, with a beacon containing 'a great bowet, with three flaming

history

archaeology

previous archaeological work and chance finds

A *East North Street / Castle Street* NJ *949 064*

probable nineteenth-century levelling
A new main sewer trench was cut across the car-park area between East North Street and Castle Street. Archaeological observation has shown that, over the whole area, the existing surface lies directly on top of natural sand and gravel. The only intrusions into the natural subsoil were modern drains; no medieval or post-medieval material was observed at all. The lack of any soil overlying the sand and gravel suggests that this area had been comprehensively levelled on some previous occasion, possibly to provide gravel for the building up of Union Street in the nineteenth century.[11]

note

11   Murray, J C, 113.

lights' to guide ships into Aberdeen harbour.[6] The seventeenth century saw it functioning as a place for ceremonial laying-out of the dead, such as Bishop Patrick Forbes in 1635 and the Marchioness of Huntly in 1638, and then as a venue for the Commissary Court,[7] for which the town council purchased a bell.[8] In 1654, the Castle Hill, enclosing the chapel, was surrounded by the English with a wall of lime and stone, part of which was quarried from the chancel of the Cathedral of St Machar. What are reputed to be some of these fortifications are still extant to the south of Castle Hill and the originals are delineated on Parson Gordon's 1661 map of Aberdeen **figure 6**. By 1659, the English troops were evicted 'to the great joy and ease of all the citizens'. The chapel, thereafter, functioned in several capacities until 1794 when it was demolished to make way for barracks,[9] which were in due course replaced by modern tower block flats.[10] To date no archaeological evidence of this structure has been discovered.

There are no historic standing buildings in Area 5 which fall within the scope of this survey.

notes

1	*ER*, i, 12.	4	Robertson, 218.
2	Gordon, in *Aberdeen Description*, 13, states 'The kings of Scotland built a castell upon the castelhill to quhat purpose it is not easie to conjecture, being that ther is no water to be found about, tho never so deepe digged.'	5	*Aberdeen Description*, 13; Fraser, *Historical Aberdeen*, 31.
		6	Robertson, 219.
		7	*Ibid*, 219, 220.
		8	*MS Council Records*, liii, 239.
		9	Robertson, 221–22.
		10	*See also* Fraser, *Thesis*.
history	3	*Rotuli Scotiae*, i, 55.	

56

area 6
Union Terrace, Denburn, and Belmont Street **figure 23**

historic sites and monuments known from documentary and cartographic sources

No historic sites and monuments known from documentary and cartographic sources are thought to have existed within Area 6. Nor are there any historic standing buildings in Area 6 which fall within the scope of this survey.

archaeological potential and future development

No archaeological excavations have so far taken place in Area 6. Against this background, basic archaeological monitoring of any episodes of ground disturbance or development will be useful. In particular, ground disturbance in *the area between Back Wynd and Belmont Street* should be carefully observed (*see* **area 7** for evidence of a medieval pit, possibly associated with farming, found at *4–6 Little Belmont Street*). It has already been decided that the planned conversion of the site of the former Aberdeen Academy in the Belmont Street/Schoolhill area will be preceded by archaeological evaluation.

Current plans to build over the Denburn dual carriageway, in the area of Union Terrace Gardens, may cause further destruction of deposits very close to the supposed western edge of the burgh. Opportunities should be taken to observe and record any archaeological deposits within the *Union Terrace Gardens/Denburn area*.

---

previous archaeological work and chance finds

A *Denburn road construction NJ 939 061–937 064 (see also* **area 2***)*

no archaeological results
Observation during road building revealed no archaeological deposits.[1]

note

1   Further information from Arts and   and Museums, Art Gallery,
     Recreation Department, Arts   Schoolhill, Aberdeen, AB10 1FQ

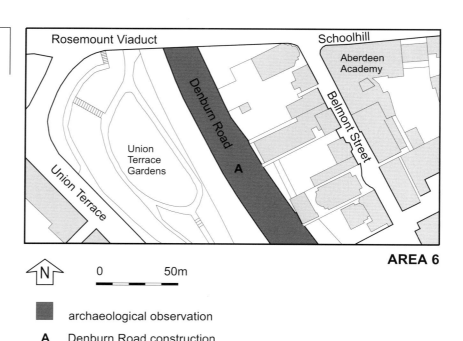

figure 23
Area 6
© Crown Copyright

AREA 6

N   0   50m

■ archaeological observation

A Denburn Road construction

area 7

Back Wynd to Netherkirkgate, including St Nicholas Church, part of Schoolhill, and the junction of Union Street and St Nicholas Street **figure 24**

historic sites and monuments known from documentary and cartographic sources

the Song School

The Song School had close links with the church, its purpose being not only to give basic instruction to pupils, but particularly to provide able songsters for St Nicholas Church. The first documentary evidence of the Song School occurs in 1483 when Richard Boyle, a chaplain at St Nicholas Church was master, although it was probably of earlier origin.[1] The school stood on the west wall of St Nicholas Churchyard, on the east side of Back Wynd. After the Reformation the school fell into decline and the master of the school fled; but in 1570 the town appointed a new master. The school, renamed the 'Musick School', was removed in 1594, on the construction of Wester Kirkgate (Back Wynd), to St Ninian's Chapel on Castle Hill for a few years (*see* **area 5**).[2] It was variously relocated until 1749 when the town ceased to maintain it.[3] To date there is no archaeological evidence of this structure.

St Thomas the Martyr Hospital

This stood in the Netherkirkgate near the east end of St Nicholas Church and to the west of the burn flowing from the Upper Mill. It was founded in May 1459 by John Clat for

---

archaeological potential and future development

Although much of this area has been developed in recent years, clearly it retains some archaeological potential, especially in and around *St Nicholas Church*. Every opportunity should be taken to test the hypothesis that a church might have existed on this site from earlier than the twelfth century, and archaeological evidence for the history of the church from the twelfth century onwards might survive concealed within its fabric or beneath its floors or in the churchyard. Any future construction work within St Nicholas Church itself or within the churchyard must be subject to prior archaeological investigation. Indeed, any development work within Area 7 will require careful archaeological observation, given the nature and number of sites and monuments presently known from documentary and cartographic sources only (*eg the Song School, House of Correction, Netherkirkgate Port, St Thomas the Martyr Hospital*, and the *Upper and Mid Mill*). The discovery of no less than four *medieval coin hoards* in this area is a potent reminder of the potential for significant archaeological finds to be recovered by chance.

Further plans to develop a site in *Broad Street, south of St Nicholas House*, will destroy an area of Broad Street frontage north-west of the site of proven archaeological wealth at *16–18 Netherkirkgate*, excavated in 1992 (*see below*). Indeed, most episodes of archaeological work which have taken place here, even in parts of the area which proved to have been disturbed by more recent activities, have yielded useful archaeological information to a greater or lesser extent (*see below*).

previous archaeological work and chance finds

A *St Nicholas Church NJ 940 062* **figure 25**

twelfth-century foundations, later medieval tomb
Excavations took place in Collison's Aisle (north transept) and the north half of the crossing prior to installation of a heating system in 1974. A coin of David I (1145–53),[26] found in the foundation of the north-west pier of the tower, suggested a twelfth-century

the care of the poor and infirm,[4] and continued in use until the late eighteenth century.[5] It may have been one and the same as the Maison Dieu referred to in September 1459 in St Nicholas Cartulary.[6] To date there is no direct archaeological evidence of this structure (*but see* St Nicholas Triangle, *below*).

a *Upper Mill, Flourmill Brae*

The Upper Mill was in existence by the fourteenth century as a meal mill, and may have been one of the 'town's mills' in need of repair in 1407 (p 17). It was sited in what became Flourmill Brae, which is now below St Nicholas Centre. The mill is seen clearly on Parson Gordon's map of 1661 **figure 6** and it continued to work until 1865. The excavated site at 43–57 Upperkirkgate, apparently located close to the mill site, produced no relevant archaeological material (though it was of archaeological importance in other respects; *see* **area 3**, p 44).

b *Mid Mill*

The Mid Mill in the Green was in existence from 1619 (*see* p 17). On a line with present Union Street, it functioned firstly as a meal mill and later as a malt mill, until 1798 when plans were made for its removal for the creation of Union Street. To date there is no archaeological evidence of this structure.

Netherkirkgate Port

This port controlled entrance to the town on the north side of St Katherine's Hill via Putachieside and the Green. To date there is no archaeological evidence of this structure (for further information on ports and the town defences, *see* pp 11–13).

g *Benholm's Lodge (Wallace Tower)*

This town house, constructed in Netherkirkgate around the year 1600, was dismantled in 1965 to make way for the present Marks and Spencers store and re-erected in Seaton Park (*see* **area 19**).

h *House of Correction*

To encourage vagabonds off the streets, in 1636 the town council had built a House of Correction 'for all idle persons and vagabonds able to work'.[7] To date there is no direct archaeological evidence of this structure (*but see* St Nicholas Triangle, *below*).

history

archaeology

date for at least that portion of the building. Later features included the base of a tomb, possibly that of Provost Davidson who died in 1411.[27]

B *human remains*

In 1990, disturbed human remains were discovered by workmen during alterations to the heating system, in an area adjacent to that excavated in 1974.[28]

C *St Nicholas Church oil pipe trench NJ 940 062*

human remains, disturbed deposits
Archaeological observation of the insertion of a narrow installation trench along the north exterior of the East Church revealed disturbed deposits and some scattered human bones only.

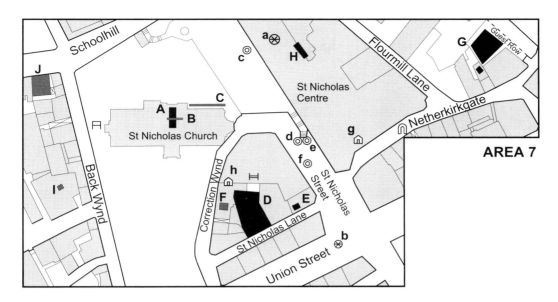

AREA 7

archaeological excavation

archaeological observation

- **A** St Nicholas Church 1974
- **B** St Nicholas Church 1992
- **C** St Nicholas Church oil pipe trench
- **D** St Nicholas Triangle
- **E** St Nicholas Triangle
- **F** 12a - 13 Correction Wynd
- **G** 16 - 18 Netherkirkgate
- **H** 43 - 57 Upperkirkgate
- **I** 4 - 6 Little Belmont Street
- **J** 45 - 51 Schoolhill

⊗ site of mill
- **a** Upper Mill
- **b** Mid Mill

◎ site of coin hoard
- **c** 1807 coin hoard
- **d** St Nicholas Street coin hoard
- **e** St Nicholas Street coin hoard
- **f** 1807 coin hoard

⌂ site of historic house
- **g** Benholm's Lodge
- **h** House of Correction

⊓ site of Song School

⋒ site of Netherkirkgate Port

⊨ site of St Thomas the Martyr Hospital

figure 24
Area 7
© Crown Copyright

history

water supply

The precise line of the water-course which led to the Mid Mill is not clear. Documentary and cartographic evidence suggests that a mill dam crossed over Upperkirkgate near to the port (*see* **area 3**), and then passed at least some of the length of the west end of tofts on Guest Row (*see* **figure 5**). Whether part of the water course continued the full length of the

archaeology

D *&* **E** *St Nicholas Triangle NJ 941 062*

truncated medieval pits, pre nineteenth-century topography
This triangular area, according to Parson Gordon's map of Aberdeen, 1661 **figure 6**, included the approximate sites of both St Thomas' Hospital (1459) and the House of Correction (1636). Excavation indicated that there had been severe disturbance to the area caused by nineteenth-century building construction, so that few deposits survived above the level of the natural subsoil. Traces of medieval pits and a post-medieval clay-bonded wall had survived, however. Nonetheless, data were obtained regarding the hitherto unexplored pre nineteenth-century topography of this area adjacent to the parish church of St Nicholas and the millburn.[29]

back tofts of Guest Row and Netherkirkgate, or was entirely redirected westwards to supply the Upper Mill in the first instance, is not clear. To date there is no archaeological evidence of the lines of water-courses (for further information on water supply, *see* pp 15–17.)

historic standing buildings

St Nicholas Church

The origins of the Church of St Nicholas are uncertain. It is first noted in a papal bull of Pope Adrian IV in 1157.[8] Although some doubts have been placed on the authenticity of this document,[9] archaeological evidence does suggest that the church was at least a twelfth-century foundation,[10] and a church may have existed on this site from much earlier times.

The siting of the church, on high ground overlooking the Green and to the west of the medieval urban nucleus, outside the town ports, has been the subject of some discussion. However, the positioning of the parish church outwith the main urban settlement is in itself not unusual: St Mary's Church, Dundee, for example, was similarly placed and other examples may also be noted in Crail and Edinburgh. A parish church was not of necessity an urban parish church; rural parishes might pre-date urban growth.

Gordon of Rothiemay gives a description of a church built in 1060, but offers no independent evidence in support.[11] It is, however, possible that St Nicholas Church was founded on the site of an earlier Christian establishment or even one of pre-Christian origin with religious associations, but there is no historical or archaeological evidence to support or disprove this theory. The dedication might suggest that the church which was in existence by the twelfth century was founded in the late eleventh century and served a community engaged in overseas trading. Berwick, Newcastle, Amsterdam, Kiel and Hamburg, all North Sea trading communities, also favoured St Nicholas as their patron saint. Perhaps this small seafaring settlement clustered near the church and extended southwards to the base of St Katherine's Hill, at the eastern end of the later-named Green. The church would, therefore, have been in close proximity to the early nucleus, and only with expansion eastwards would the parish church appear to take on the nature of an extra-urban establishment. An alternative theory is that St Nicholas was carved out of St Machar's Parish by the allocation of 800 acres, leaving 3200 acres for the parent parish, at a time when the small trading settlement on the banks of the Dee had grown sufficiently to merit a parish separate from that of St Machar two miles further north. The new church was of necessity on a peripheral site either because there was an insufficiency of gap sites for building in the centre or because the bishop chose to place the church on land already

history · in his possession.[12]

archaeology

F *12a–13 Correction Wynd NJ 941 062*

no archaeological results
During conversion work, two small trial trenches were excavated through the floor of the standing building. They revealed that the existing ground level of the building was semi-cellared and cut into natural subsoil, any occupation layers having been destroyed previously. Observation of the small yard at the rear of the property also revealed no undisturbed levels.[30]

G *16–18 Netherkirkgate NJ 942 083*

medieval and post-medieval buildings, fences, organic deposits
Redevelopment of a portion of the frontage of Broad Street/Guest Row provided an opportunity to examine a site on the west side of this street. A small section of the available area had been completely destroyed by cellar activity, but the remainder of the

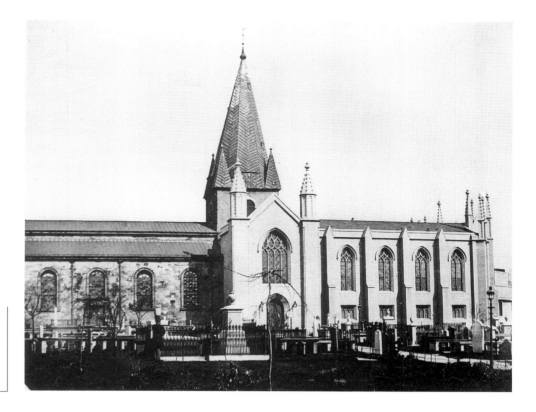

figure 25
Steeple of
St Nicholas Church
prior to its
destruction by fire

The earliest surviving architectural remains, dating from the late twelfth century, point to a church building consisting of an aisled nave, with north and south transepts, topped by a central tower, the east end being furnished with an aisled chancel of three bays and ending in a semi-circular apse. The transepts were extended to the south in 1355, and about this time a chapel was apparently added to the east side of the north transept, resulting in the blocking of one window and the insertion of a doorway in the east wall.[13] There is reference to a chapel in 1445 when it was known as the vault of 'Our Lady of Pity'. The appellation 'St Mary' in Gordon charters occurs as later additions in blank spaces.[14]

A new choir was begun *c* 1477 and John Fendour's craftsmanship was exhibited here. In 1495 money was lent to the town council 'to pay Johne Fendour for the makeing of the ruff and tymmer of the queyr',[15] and by 1508 he was to receive £200 Scots and a bounty if by Michaelmas 1508 he had completed his work, which was to 'big, oupmak, and finally end and complet the xxxiiij stallis in thar queir, with the spiris and the chanslar dur, and ale uther thingis according tharto'.[16] A further improvement was an oak-built steeple over the main body of the church, which was to survive until destroyed by fire in 1874 **figure 25**.

history

archaeology

area was comparatively undisturbed. A large area of undisturbed medieval organic material was excavated, containing considerable quantities of wood, bone, a fine collection of textiles, and pottery. It is rare for organic materials to survive at all, especially medieval textiles, which makes this an important assemblage. Evidence of buildings was found in two parts of the site. On the Guest Row frontage there were portions of post-medieval stone foundations. Towards the rear of the site a range of post-holes possibly indicated remains of one or more medieval wooden buildings. Other post and stake alignments were readily open to interpretation as fences or boundaries. There was also a large number of medieval and post-medieval pits. Large medieval pits lay adjacent to and underneath the present street frontage of Guest Row.[31]

H *43–57 Upperkirkgate NJ 941 063 (see also* **area 3***)*

fifteenth- to sixteenth-century buildings
This site on the south side of Upperkirkgate produced evidence of thirteenth- to

The medieval parish church of St Nicholas was not only one of the largest burgh churches in Scotland, being 256 ft (78 m) long, but also one of the most prestigious. In 1256, the parochial revenues of St Nicholas were assigned to the sixth prebend of the Cathedral of St Machar.[17] The church housed a number of altars and chaplainries. By 1450, ten chaplainries had been endowed: the cordiners endowed St Crispin's in 1495; the masons that of St John the Baptist; and the hammermen supported the altar of St Eloiryne.[18] In 1491 the number of chaplains was twenty-two.[19] This may soon have been reduced to sixteen,[20] although thirty-four stalls were ordered for the new choir on its construction in 1507.[21] As the number of chaplainries grew, there developed a college of chaplains which preceded the constitution of St Nicholas as a collegiate church by at least a century. It was not until 1540, with the granting of the vicarage of St Nicholas to 'the college of the chaplenis of ... Sanct Nicholas Kirk ... for sustenation of ane provost', that full collegiate status was achieved.[22]

The church was further supported by the town, local gentry, and nobility with grants of rentals, endowments of chaplainries and other gifts. Burgesses also gave of their skills in the repair and adornment of the church. The St Nicholas Cartulary gives indications of the many gifts to the church in the form of lands or rents, bells, chalices and the like. William Leth, for example, donated two bells and Ralph Voket repainted the image of St Nicholas; Sir John Rutherfurd granted valuable rents between 1489 and 1506 from various Aberdeen tenements.[23] From the fifteenth century there is evidence of money raised by the town authorities for the 'kirk wark': for example, funds were assigned from the town fishings to pay for choir fittings in 1477; £35 was raised in 1500 towards the cost of lead for the church and its transport from Berwick on Tweed to Aberdeen; and, again, in 1513 a further £74 was donated for improvments to the church fabric.[24]

Despite a conservative rearguard action after the Reformation, St Nicholas Church by the 1580s was stripped of most of its Catholic furnishings. In 1596, it was divided into two separate churches, serving two different parishes. The nave housed a large congregation throughout part of the seventeenth century. By 1732, however, it had become so ruinous that it had to be abandoned. It was occupied by the Duke of Cumberland's troops in 1746, and was rebuilt between 1750 and 1755 to a design by James Gibb when it was re-opened as the West Church. The choir was divided from the transept by a stone wall after the Reformation and housed a separate congregation as the New Church. It was rebuilt in 1837 as the East Church, but burned down in 1874 and was re-opened in 1876.

Most of the surviving evidence of the twelfth-century work is in the north transept, now called Collison's Aisle. This is one of the most significant medieval remnants of New

history

archaeology

twentieth-century activity. Cellarage and road widening had destroyed any traces of street frontage deposits, but remains of some fifteenth- to sixteenth-century buildings had survived. No evidence was found of the Upper Mill, nor of the possible 'defensive bank' visible on Parson Gordon's map of 1661 (*see* **figure 6**).

| *4–6 Little Belmont Street* NJ 940 062

thirteenth- to fourteenth-century pit, ?medieval farm
This site was archaeologically observed while the foundations of an extension to Cameron's Inn were being excavated. Below the yard surface there was an homogeneous loam (interpreted as cultivated earth), containing a small assemblage of medieval and post-medieval pottery. A small oval pit, sealed by the cultivated soil and cut into natural subsoil, was filled with charcoal-rich soil and burnt clay and contained mid thirteenth- to early fourteenth-century pottery, including fabrics from Yorkshire. The location of a medieval pit here, well to the west of the Upperkirkgate Port and outside the town boundary, suggests some form of sub-urban medieval occupation, possibly associated with a farm.[32]

Aberdeen. The transept was remodelled in the seventeenth century, but, despite alterations, the exterior walls show the series of characteristic round-headed, deep-splayed windows, now blocked up, and there are two small archways which led to the main aisle. This transitional-style architecture dates to the late twelfth or early thirteenth century, and is further evidenced in the four arches under the central tower and clerestory windows in the east and west walls of the aisle, one of which has angle shafts with carved cap and mouldings.[25]

The mortuary or chantry chapel of the Gordon family, or vault of 'Our Lady of Pity', was designed on a three-bay plan, with rib and groin vault, and now houses fine examples of fifteenth- and sixteenth-century woodwork, some executed by John Fendour. It is now known as St Mary's chapel, and may be entered from Correction Wynd.

Some archaeological evidence has been recovered from St Nicholas Church, including twelfth-century foundations, a later medieval tomb and human remains (*see below*).

notes

1	*St Nich Cart*, ii, 335.	16	*Ibid*, 102.
2	Milne, 51–2.	17	*Abdn Reg*, ii, 40.
3	*See also* Fraser, *Thesis*.	18	Kennedy, ii, 13–38, contains a list of the charities involved.
4	*St Nich Cart*, ii, *no* lxxxiv.		
5	Milne, 91.	29	*St Nich Cart*, ii, 229–30.
6	Fraser, *Thesis*, 85–96.	20	*Ibid*, 231.
7	*Council Register, Extracts*, 1625–1642, 106.	21	*Ibid*, 346.
8	*St Nich Cart*, vii–ix.	22	*Ibid*, ii, 381; Cowan and Easson, 215; Milne, 74. The college of St Nicholas is discussed in detail in Fraser, *Thesis*.
9	Milne, 70.		
10	Murray, J C, 246.		
11	*Aberdeen Description*, 14.	23	*Abdn Reg*, i, 35; *St Nich Cart*, ii, 180; ii, 12–17; Ewan, 35; *MS Sasine Register*, i, 198; ii, 199; iii, 34. Thanks are due to Dr H Booton for these references.
12	Cripps, J, 'Establishing the topography of medieval Aberdeen', in Smith, *New Light*, 5; Hunter, 105.		
13	Hunter, 238.	24	*Aberdeen Council Register*, i, 83; i, 68; i, 85–7.
14	Iain Fraser, *pers comm.*		
15	*Burgh Records, Extracts (a)*, 56.	25	Hunter, 238.

history

archaeology

J 45–51 Schoolhill NJ 940 063

excavation of frontage site
During construction work on this frontage site within the confines of the medieval burgh, an area measuring 275 sq m was exposed, of which the front portion (up to 14 m from the street) was cellared. At the rear up to 0.60 m of deposits were observed, but no finds were recognised.[33]

c–f *St Nicholas Street NJ 941 062*

medieval coin hoards
Aberdeen is probably unique in Europe in the number and size of its medieval coin hoards. No fewer than five have been unearthed in the city centre with another two having been uncovered in the Futty area (*see* **areas 3**, **4** *&* **5**, and **gazetteer**). Four of the five city-centre hoards were found in the area of St Nicholas Street **figure 26**. The two earliest discoveries, both made in 1807[34] (**c** *&* **f** on **figure 24**) consisted mainly of English silver pennies of the thirteenth and fourteenth centuries. The first of these was apparently contained in a large wooden bowl but its size is unknown; the second contained around

64

figure 26

St Nicholas Street
coin hoards

archaeology

1,800 coins in a pottery jar. As well as pennies, the first hoard seems to have included some groats.[35]

The above grid reference locates the position of two more recent hoards, found only 3.5 m apart beneath St Nicholas Street in 1983 and 1984, during construction of the St Nicholas Centre (**d** *&* **e**). They were similar in composition to the earlier finds except for the fact that no groats were present. Their contents totalled 4,493 and 2,538 silver pennies respectively. Both hoards had been deposited in the ground in locally-made pottery jugs.[36]

notes

26 The coin is in very poor condition, and was previously wrongly identified as Malcolm IV.
27 Hunter, 242.
28 *Ibid*, 236–247; *see also Discovery and Excavation in Scotland 1990*, 17.
29 Cameron, *St Nicholas*.
30 Murray, J C, 113.
31 Cameron, *Netherkirkgate*, and Cameron, *Netherkirkgate* (forthcoming).

32 Murray, J C, 112–113.
33 Further information from Arts and Recreation Department, Arts and Museums, Art Gallery, Schoolhill, Aberdeen, AB10 1FQ.
34 Evans and Thain, 327–44.
35 *Ibid*, 330; Mayhew, 1988, 40–68.
36 *See* Evans and Thain.

area 8

Broad Street, Union Street, Castle Street, King Street **figure 27**

historic sites and monuments known from documentary and cartographic sources

a *Laird of Pitfoddels' House, Castle Street*

Built about 1530, this house stood on the south side of Castlegate, to the west of the Earl Marischal's house. It consisted of three floors and was turreted for ornament and defence. The Marquis of Huntly used it for his residence in 1639 at the commencement of the Wars of the Covenant and Charles II may also have stayed here in 1650. The house was demolished in the early nineteenth century. To date there is no archaeological evidence of this structure, though excavations at *no* 3 Bonded Warehouse, Virginia Street (Area 11), may have investigated part of the garden to the rear of this house.

b *Earl Marischal's House, Castle Street*

The house stood on the south side of Castlegate, on a site at the north end of the present Marischal Street. Clearly visible on Gordon's map of 1661 **figure 6**, it consisted of a number of buildings of two storeys height around a central court. The large gardens attached to it extended to approximately the line of Virginia Street. It was said to have been visited by Mary Queen of Scots in 1562. The house was purchased by the town council in the mid eighteenth century for £800 and was ultimately demolished to make way for Marischal Street. The archaeological site at *no* 3 Bonded Warehouse, Virginia Street (*see* **area 11**), lay west of what may have been the garden of this house.

---

archaeological potential and future development

Much of this important area has already been redeveloped and there have been relatively few opportunities for archaeological excavation and recording. Nonetheless, excavations in *Queen Street* and *Broad Street* have produced well-stratified evidence of twelfth- to fourteenth-century wooden buildings and other activities (*see below*); and a more recent watching brief during renovation works to the *tolbooth* produced important evidence of the history and decoration of this late medieval building. Clearly, any further works in or beneath the tolbooth will also require archaeological observation. The discovery of a complete medieval jug in King Street is a reminder of the potential for important finds to be discovered by chance.

In parts of Area 8, some archaeological potential remains. Any future development proposals in Area 8 are likely to require careful monitoring and, in some cases, there is likely to be a requirement for excavation. No specific sites are the subject of development proposals at present.

previous archaeological work and chance finds

A *2–28 Queen Street NJ 943 063*

medieval clay-bonded foundations
Excavation in this area yielded the remains of two clay-bonded stone foundations which appeared to be of medieval date.[9]

B *Queen Street Midden Area NJ 943 063*

thirteenth- to fifteenth-century evidence, pits, wattle and sill beam structures
Excavation revealed that an early thirteenth-century domestic settlement was followed in

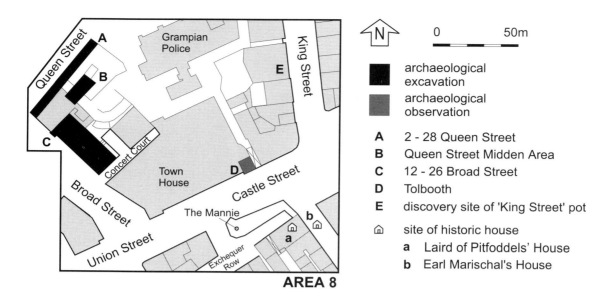

AREA 8

N

0   50m

■ archaeological excavation

▓ archaeological observation

A 2 - 28 Queen Street
B Queen Street Midden Area
C 12 - 26 Broad Street
D Tolbooth
E discovery site of 'King Street' pot

⌂ site of historic house
    a Laird of Pitfoddels' House
    b Earl Marischal's House

figure 27
Area 8
© Crown Copyright

water supply

It has been suggested (although there is no archaeological or documentary evidence to support this) that an early medieval water supply passed down Guest Row[1] and ran a mill at the foot of Guest Row and Broad Street. It was said to then pass under Exchequer Row and down the steep slope to Denburn. If this supposition had been correct, an invaluable water system would have been supplied to the Castlegate area, which had no such natural resources. It was not until the eighteenth century that water was finally piped into the central areas of the town, and even this proved not fully adequate.[2] A main 'fountain' was, however, erected in Castlegate in 1706, fed from lead pipes from Carden's Well, surmounted by a temporary wooden figure which was replaced by a lead statue, 'the Mannie'. In 1852, this was moved to the Green, but was re-erected once more in the twentieth century, in the Castlegate where it still stands (*see* pp 15–17 for further information on water supplies).[3]

historic standing buildings

tolbooth

history

The tolbooth stood close by the market place from the fifteenth century. It was here, as well as at the town ports, that the dues were paid by all entering with goods to benefit from the burgh market. The town weights would be housed in the tolbooth and the public

archaeology

the second half of the century by the digging of a series of cess and rubbish pits. This may indicate the increased formalisation of the Broad Street frontage properties by the second half of the thirteenth century, the backlands then being used for the disposal of domestic and commercial waste. In the late thirteenth or early fourteenth century, a wooden structure was in use, its archaeological remains comprising wattle and daub, a possible sill beam and substantial post pits. No fifteenth- to seventeenth-century levels survived.[10]

C *12–26 Broad Street NJ 943 063*

twelfth- to fourteenth-century wooden buildings
Excavation at this site produced evidence of plot division from the late twelfth or early thirteenth century, and the remains of wooden buildings representing some five phases of construction between the late twelfth and fourteenth centuries. The best-preserved building arrangements were dated to the fourteenth century. There was evidence of the use of sill beam construction, of stone foundations and of post-and-wattle.[11]

figure 28
Seventeenth-century
decoration
in the tolbooth

weigh-beam or tron stood nearby. The tolbooth, as in other burghs, also functioned as the meeting place for the burgh council and as the town gaol. When Robert II sanctioned the erection of a tolbooth in 1393 it was specifically required that this should not be placed within the open market place.[4] There are no firm details of the structure of this building other than that it had a steeple. The tolbooth was constructed sometime after 1407 when it was determined that each man of Aberdeen should by rotation give a day's labour *ad pretorium* or pay four pence.[5] By 1530, the citizens were able to keep watch for the safety of their town from the steeples of St Nicholas Church and the tolbooth. In 1589, both steeples were blown down.[6]

history

archaeology

D *Tolbooth NJ 945 064*

?basement cell, seventeenth-century wall decoration
Renovation work within the Town House complex since 1989 has allowed previously unseen above- and below-ground archaeological evidence of the tolbooth to be recovered. When the floor in the entrance hall off Castle Street was removed in 1989, glimpses were seen of a possible additional cell below the present floor level. Removal of wall surfaces in the entrance hall uncovered elements of an elaborate seventeenth-century decoration scheme **figure 28**, while elsewhere part of the outer face of the tolbooth's east wall was exposed.[12]

E *King Street NJ 944 064*

complete medieval jug (chance find)
A complete late thirteenth-century jug of local manufacture was found during construction work at *no* 13 King Street in 1872.[13] Rediscovered at that same address over 100 years later, it was purchased by the City of Aberdeen in 1994.

68

In 1615, a square tower with corbelled bartizans was added, to function as a wardhouse. This replaced much of the fifteenth-century tolbooth. A steeple and belfry were built in 1627. Much of the tolbooth was demolished in the nineteenth century, leaving the wardhouse standing, but the building was still referred to as the tolbooth. The present tower, which is now open as a civic museum, dates from 1726.[17] Recent conversion work within the present tolbooth allowed limited archaeological excavation and recording of above- and below-ground archaeological evidence for this structure (*see below*).

It is possible that there was also an earlier tolbooth. Gordon maintains that this was sited near to the shore, at the west end of present Virginia Street (*see* **area 11**).[8]

notes

history

1 Guest Row, which once ran parallel to Broad Street on its west side, was largely obliterated by the construction of St Nicholas House. A remnant of it can be seen in Area 7. *See also* conjectural sketch map **figure 5**.

2 Milne, 109, 115.
3 Fraser, *Green*, 32.
4 *Abdn Chrs*, xv.
5 *Abdn Recs*, i, 238.
6 Wyness, 145; Robertson, 195.
7 Brogden, 8.
8 *Aberdeen Description*, 9.

archaeology notes

9 Murray, J C, 18–19.
10 *Ibid*, 20–25.
11 *Ibid*, 12–26.
12 *See Discovery and Excavation in Scotland 1990*, 17. Drawings of these discoveries are held by RCAHMS and Arts and Recreation Department, Arts

and Museums, Art Gallery, Schoolhill, Aberdeen, AB10 1FQ.

13 *Aberdeen Journal*, 20 March 1872, page 6, col 4; further information from Arts and Recreation Department, Arts and Museums, Art Gallery, Schoolhill, Aberdeen, AB10 1FQ.

area 9
Castle Street, Castle Terrace, Virginia Street **figure 29**

historic sites and monuments known from documentary and cartographic sources

a *Futty Port*

This port stood at the south-east of Castlegate on Futty Wynd, controlling access to the Castlegate. It was probably in existence from the fifteenth century at latest.

b *Justice Port*

Futty Port's control of entrance to the Castlegate was reinforced by a further port at the north-eastern corner of Castlegate—the Justice or Thieves Port, so named from its site on the street leading to the seat of the Justiciar's Circuit Courts beside Castle Hill, or from the thieves, sentenced to be hanged, passing through this port to Heading Hill.[1] Repairs to the port were effected during the sixteenth century. Its removal was ordered in 1769, although it remained standing because its west wall formed the gable of a house that encroached on the south side of the street. It was finally demolished in 1787.[2]

   To date there is no archaeological evidence for either the Futty or Justice Ports. (*See* pp 11–13 for further information on the town's ports).

Knights' Templar property

The Knights Templar held land in the north-eastern corner of Castle Street, but there is no evidence that they had a convent and church.

---

archaeological potential and future development

This area has produced a wide variety of archaeological deposits and features in previous investigations (*see below*), including the debris of medieval craft activities such as bronze-working, gravel quarrying, medieval and later pathways, the remains of timbers, property divisions, and post-medieval structures. The variability of archaeological survival has at times been surprising, with examination of a site at *nos 6–8 Castle Terrace*, for instance, proving relatively productive archaeologically, and yet examination of a nearby site, at *42 Castle Street*, yielding nothing of archaeological interest. Previous work at Albion Court, 18 Castle Street, has demonstrated that the archaeological interest of post-medieval and early modern Aberdeen should not be forgotten.

   Continued archaeological monitoring will be required routinely in this area, and, in particular, any proposed ground disturbance to the *north of Castle Street* and to the *south of Virginia Street* will require an archaeological response. No sites in this area are known to be under threat from development proposals at present.

previous archaeological work and chance finds

A *Albion Court, 18 Castle Street NJ 945 064*

seventeenth-century terrace
At this site the opportunity was taken to record one of the last surviving terraces of buildings which pre-date the nineteenth-century 'granite city' and to put the buildings into a dated context through excavation. A good range of clay pipes, coins and pottery highlighted the connections enjoyed by Aberdeen with the Low Countries in the sixteenth and seventeenth centuries.[5]

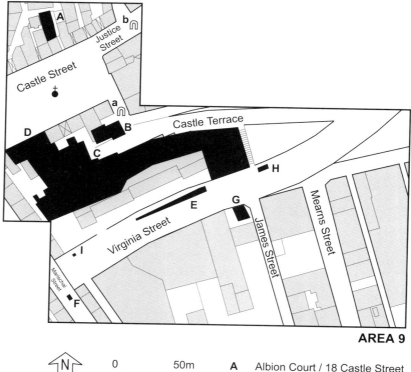

AREA 9

N   0   50m

■   archaeological excavation

∩   site of port
a   Futty Port
b   Justice Port

✝   Market Cross

A   Albion Court / 18 Castle Street
B   6 - 8 Castle Terrace
C   south side Castle Street sites
D   42 Castle Street
E   27 - 37 Virginia Street
F   Bannerman's Bridge
G   42 Virginia Street
H   Virginia Street steps
I   17 Virginia Street

figure 29
Area 9
© Crown Copyright

historic standing buildings

burgh market

history

The medieval market was held in Castle Street. A market here was recommended partly by the nature of the street: Gordon describes it as 'a squair, about a hundred walking

archaeology

B *6–8 Castle Terrace* NJ *945 063*

seventeenth-century smithy, gravel quarrying
Medieval activity on this site had been almost totally destroyed by scarping and by later intrusive features, but evidence of the later development of the site survived. In the seventeenth century a small workshop, possibly a smithy, was constructed. At a later stage, gravel quarrying took place; finally, the area was cleared and became a yard attached to an early eighteenth-century mansion.[6]

C *south side Castle Street* NJ *945 063*

thirteenth- to twentieth-century dumping and other activities
Excavations to the south and east of *nos 6–8 Castle Terrace* site (*see above*) revealed traces of thirteenth- to twentieth-century land use. In the earliest period there was evidence of

figure 30
The market cross
in Castle Street,
built in 1686 and
moved to its present
location in 1842

paces in breadth and twyce as much in lenthe; nor can Scotland show such ane other',[3] but also because of its close proximity to the harbour, via Shiprow. Aberdeen market served not only the sea-borne export and import trade, but also functioned as an entrepôt and distribution centre for the rural hinterland around New Aberdeen.

market crosses

The market cross, later named the Flesh Cross, stood in front of the tolbooth (*see* Area 8), which was on the site of the present day Town House, and in due course a fish cross stood further east in approximately the position of the extant market cross **figure 30**. The extant cross is a fine example of an early market cross. Above its arcade is a parapet divided into twelve panels; these contain armorial bearings of the Crown and the City, as well as bas-relief portraits of the Stewart monarchs from James I to James VII. A column with Corinthian cap, wreathed by thistles and roses in bas-relief, supports a coloured and gilt marble unicorn.[4] The market cross was built in 1686 and was moved to the quieter end of the square in 1842. It is a scheduled ancient monument.

history   *harbour (see* **area 12***)*

archaeology   sand quarrying, of attempts to revet the steeply sloping ground, and of rubbish dumping, specifically, in one pit, the remains of a large quantity of burnt material and fragments of bronze.

   Two sections of clay-bonded wall indicated the survival of property divisions from the fifteenth century, while an adjacent cobbled pathway, of the same date, may have been the remains of an access way from Castlegate towards the line of modern Virginia Street. Significant amounts of pottery imported from Yorkshire and continental Europe may hint at the comparative wealth of Castlegate residents in the medieval period.

D *42 Castle Street NJ 944 063*

no archaeological results
Examination of relatively undisturbed levels below one nineteenth-century frontage building at *no* 42 Castle Street revealed virtually no deposits above the natural subsoil.[7]

notes

1   Milne, 27.
2   *MS Council Records*, lxiii, 119; lxv, 184.
3   *Aberdeen Description*, 12.

4   Brogden, 7–8. The column was moved to the Tolbooth Museum in 1996, and replaced with a replica.

E *27–37 Virginia Street NJ 945 063*

thirteenth- to fourteenth-century layers, wooden posts
Excavation revealed medieval layers of sand and gravel, with the remains of wooden posts dated to the thirteenth to fourteenth century. One pit is thought to be of fifteenth- to seventeenth-century date. A stone-built clay-bonded drain was of eighteenth or nineteenth-century origin.[8]

F *Bannerman's Bridge, Virginia Street NJ 945 062*

bridge construction levels
Bannerman's Bridge was originally constructed in 1768 to carry the new Marischal Street from the high ground of the Castle Street ridge to the lower shore and harbour frontage. One trench was excavated in a chamber below the south end of the bridge, prior to major bridge works associated with the Virginia Street road-widening. Excavation revealed a wall, probably associated with the construction of the bridge, together with layers of mortar and clay. There were no medieval levels.[9]

G *42 Virginia Street NJ 946 062*

thirteenth- to eighteenth-century evidence, ?fifteenth-century building
In the thirteenth to fourteenth century, sand and clay layers were associated with the remains of wooden posts and other timbers. At a slightly later date (perhaps into the fifteenth century) an 'L'-shaped stone foundation may have been the base for a timber superstructure. An overlying cobbled surface was dated to the sixteenth to eighteenth century.[10]

H *Virginia Street steps, Castle Lane NJ 946 063*

Futty Wynd, midden deposits, clay quarrying
A small excavation took place here in 1974. Part of what was thought to be the fourteenth-century surface of Futty Wynd, the route from Castle Street to the fishing settlement of Futty, was revealed. There were also midden deposits and some possible evidence of the quarrying of clay, both earlier than the road construction.[11]

I *17 Virginia Street NJ 945 062*

no archaeological results
A small trial pit here revealed only natural levels.[12]

notes

5   Evans, 271–96.
6   Murray, J C, 100–106.
7   Further information from Arts and Recreation Department, Arts and Museums, Art Gallery, Schoolhill, Aberdeen, AB10 1FQ.

8   Stones and Cameron (forthcoming).
9   *Ibid.*
10 *Ibid.*
11 Murray, J C, 107.
12 *Ibid*, 108.

area 10

Union Street to Guild Street, including the Green, with Market Street to the east **figure 31**

historic sites and monuments known from documentary and cartographic sources

a *Trinitarian House*

The date of the foundation of a Trinitarian House in Aberdeen is uncertain. It has been claimed that in 1211 William the Lion granted his palace and gardens, to the south-west of St Katherine's Hill, to the order of Trinitarians to establish a house in Aberdeen;[1] but there is no documentary evidence to support this claim, and it is doubtful whether there was ever a royal residence to the south of the Green. Trinity friars were in Aberdeen by

archaeological potential and future development

The *Green* has been the focus of recent debates about the site of the original settlement of New Aberdeen (*see* pp 14–15). Excavations to date have not entirely resolved this argument but have shown that the area was marshy in the medieval period, highly susceptible to flooding, and consequently unfavourable to building. No early urban settlement was revealed in excavations at *2–12 Rennie's Wynd* and *67–71 Green* (*see below*), though parts of the west end of the Green were in use by the end of the twelfth century.

figure 31

Area 10

© Crown Copyright

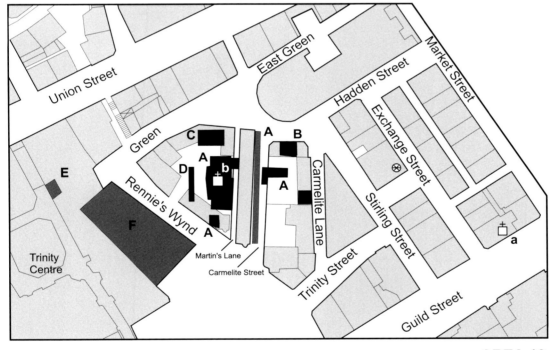

AREA 10

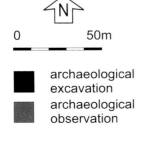

0   50m

■ archaeological excavation

▨ archaeological observation

A 12 Martin's Lane
B 19 Hadden Street
C 45 - 59 Green
D 67 - 71 Green
E 104 Green
F 2 - 12 Rennie's Wynd

⌂ site of friary
a Trinitarian House
b Carmelite Friary

⊗ site of Nether Mill

1273 at the latest, however,[2] and their choice of site, as with the Carmelite order, would suggest that the Green was not the focal point of urban settlement by this time. A community continued until the Reformation, but neither historical nor archaeological research has yet indicated the precise extent of the complex. The buildings of the Trinitarian House would appear to have been in a state of disrepair by 1560,[3] when it is said the house was sacked.[4] The following year sasine of the monastery and buildings was granted to Gilbert Menzies of Cowlie[5] and in 1632 a hospital for burgesses was founded on the site.[6] This stood until the eighteenth century and is evidenced on both Gordon's (1661: **figure 6**) and Milne's (1789) maps. The churchyard, however, appears to have been used for refuse dumping until 1606, when it was ordered that it should be cleaned up so that ship-building might proceed.[7] 'The kirkyard of the Trinitie Freris' being 'fitthilie abusit be middingis' was 'the maist meit and convenient place for bigging of a bark'.[8] Other buildings associated with the friary were purchased in the seventeenth century by Dr William Guild and granted to the Incorporated Trades of Aberdeen.[9] The Trades Hall **figure 32**, demolished in the 1840s to make way for Guild Street, may have incorporated some of the friary buildings.[10]

Although the Protestant Reformation removed much of the fabric of the Trinity House, public opinion favoured the old Catholic order to some extent, and as late as 1616 the town council granted provision for one Richard Garden 'sometime one of the Trinitie Friars'.[11] To date there is no archaeological evidence of this structure.

b *Carmelite Friary*

There were representatives of the Carmelite order in Aberdeen from the late thirteenth century. As early as 1273 a grant was made to the Carmelites 'till their buildings should be completed'.[12] Indications are that building had commenced by the end of the century;[13] and a series of grants was made to the house between 1273 and 1350 which were confirmed by David II in 1361.[14] Robert I granted annual rents to the house from the burgh fermes 'till their church be completed'.[15] This church may have been finished as late as 1355,[16] although a grant of an annual rent in that year 'for the repair of the fabric of their church' suggests an earlier date.[17]

The friary complex appears to have had the southern edge of the Green as its northern boundary, and extended east to west over Rennie's Wynd, Martin's Lane and Carmelite Street. The exact boundaries have yet to be defined, both by documentary and

history

archaeology

The location in the Green area in the thirteenth century of the houses of two important religious orders, the Trinitarians and the Carmelites, also suggests that the Green was then merely a suburb to the main nucleus of settlement. Archaeological assessment of the eastern end of the Green might have contributed evidence to this debate, whether positive or negative, but the archaeological potential of this area has been largely destroyed by development. Wherever appropriate, every opportunity should continue to be taken in the Green area to test hypotheses about the nature and siting of the earliest urban settlement, and the nature of early development in this area from the twelfth century onwards.

Other desirable archaeological themes in Area 10 include defining the extent of the *Carmelite and Trinitarian Friaries*, and reconstructing their development and land use both within and around their precincts. Despite the level of development which has already occurred, it is possible that future investigations, both beneath standing buildings and in the open spaces between them, could still yield important archaeological evidence.

Finally, the discovery of *Mesolithic material* on sites in this area, specifically, at *45–59* and *67–71 Green (below)*, is a salutary reminder that there is a recognised (though unpredictable) potential for prehistoric and other pre-urban archaeological evidence to survive in the city centre.

Archaeological monitoring of any proposed ground disturbance within this area will continue to be required as a matter of routine and occasionally archaeological excavation

figure 32

Aberdeen Trades Hall, on the site of the Trinitarian Friary, may have incorporated former friary buildings

archaeological research. The southern boundary would doubtless have been limited by the confluence of the Dee and Denburn, as there is evidence of flooding, tidal flows and water-logged conditions, unfavourable to building.[18]

The choice of this site for a Carmelite House and also the site of the Trinitarian House nearby would suggest that this area, to the west and south-west of St Katherine's Hill, was not the focal point of main urban settlement by the late thirteenth century. Regular religious orders usually chose to place their houses outwith main settlement, on the periphery of the town.

Archaeological research has shown that considerable rebuilding took place in the late fourteenth and fifteenth centuries, which would suggest a community somewhat larger than 'at least four friars' at the Reformation as evidenced in documentary sources.[19] The friary was destroyed in 1560, during the Protestant Reformation,[20] and the Carmelite property fell to the crown, thereafter to be granted to private individuals and the town council.[21] Marischal College benefited in due course by the gift of Friars' Glen in Drumtochty from the Earl Marischal[22] and in the mid seventeenth century from revenues

history

archaeology

may be necessary in advance of developments. No sites are presently under threat from proposed development.

previous archaeological work and chance finds

A *12 Martin's Lane NJ 941 060*

Carmelite Friary

Excavation here in 1980–81 revealed the site of the Carmelite Friary, founded *c* 1273. The south-west portion of a possibly fourteenth-century church was uncovered, along with fragments of window glass, stone roof tiles, lead water piping and over 120 human burials.[29]

In 1994, further excavation revealed much of the west range of the Friary, as well as the north-west corner of the church, with two moulded stones from the north doorway. In a sewer trench on the line of Carmelite Street, traces were found of what may have been the east end of the church and part of the east cloister range.[30]

Excavation took place in 1995 to east of the church, where evidence of an external burial ground was uncovered.

76

figure 33
Excavation
in progress at the
Carmelite Friary site

gifted by the daughter of the artist George Jamesone who fell heir to a portion of the Carmelite gardens.[23]

history

For archaeological evidence of the Carmelite Friary, *see 12 Martin's Lane; 19 Hadden Street; 45–59 Green and 67–71 Green, below.*

archaeology

B *19 Hadden Street NJ 941 061*

garden soil, human bones
A small excavation here suggested that this area may have been within the confines of the Carmelite Friary from the thirteenth to the sixteenth century. Substantial deposits of garden soil, containing a few scattered and fragmentary human bones, were found.[31]

C *45–59 Green NJ 941 061*

Mesolithic activity, medieval garden soil, ?Carmelite Friary precincts
Following traces of occupation of Mesolithic date (about 6,500 to 4,000 BC; literally, the Middle Stone Age)—which are very common on sites in Aberdeen city centre—the

Nether Mill (later known as Trinity Mill)

This mill can be seen clearly on Gordon's map of 1661 **figure 6**. It was constructed in 1525 to the north of the Trinitarian House, and perhaps as early as 1459, when a reference to a 'higher' mill would imply the existence of this mill lower down the watercourse. The Nether mill continued to work until 1865. To date there is no archaeological evidence of this structure.

water supply

The fifteenth-century Sasine Registers of Aberdeen hold crucial evidence on the water courses near the Trinitarian House and lower Green region, and in particular on the 'common torrent' which led from the 'aqueduct of the mills',[24] which may possibly be synonymous with the Putachie; and on the 'two torrents' that led to the Trinitarian House and the lower mill.[25] The Carmelite House was supplied with water by lead piping[26] (*see below*) and may also have used this same source of water. References, for example, to the Putachie Stream are rare in primary sources. One explanation appears in a disposition of 1741 when a Temple tenement is described as having as its western boundary 'the burn sometime called the mill burn and now Putachies burn'.[27] When this same tenement had been described in 1636,[28] for instance, as having a boundary as 'millburn' there was no indication that this was indeed the Putachie. All references to the 'mill burn', however, are not synonymous with this stream. It is clear that two, if not more, branches of the same water course were termed the 'mill burn'. A systematic assessment of the existing documentary source material could result in a precise plotting of this water course (*see* pp 15–17 for further information on the town's water supply).

There are no historic standing buildings in Area 10 which fall within the scope of this survey.

notes

1	Robertson, 26; *Aberdeen Friars*, 11, for example.
2	Cowan and Easson, 108.
3	Donaldson, 8, 97, 225; Cowan and Easson, 108.
4	Cowan and Easson, 108.
5	*Aberdeen Friars*, 98.
6	Cowan and Easson, 195.
7	*Ibid*, 108.
8	*Aberdeen Council Register*, ii, 280.
9	Milne, 70.
10	Stones, *Two Burghs*, 22.
11	Fraser, *Green*, 21.
12	*Aberdeen Friars*, 12; Cowan and Easson, 135.
13	*Aberdeen Friars*, 12.
14	*Ibid*, 12–17; Cowan and Easson, 135.
15	*Aberdeen Friars*, 14.
16	Stones, *Friaries*.

history

archaeology

earliest signs of activity on this site were a patch of cobbles and some burnt material dating to the late twelfth or early thirteenth century, succeeded by some slightly later post-holes. These features were overlain by garden soil which had accumulated between the fourteenth and eighteenth centuries. Later features included an eighteenth-century drain, but nineteenth-century cellarage had destroyed many deposits. It was concluded that this area lay within the confines of the Carmelite Friary until the Reformation, and had seen little development through much of the medieval period.[32]

D *67–71 Green NJ 940 060*

Mesolithic activity, medieval garden soil, ?Carmelite Friary precincts
This site also produced evidence of Mesolithic activity. There were indications of

history

17 *RMS*, i, *no* 259; Cowan and Easson, 135.

18 Murray, J C, 95.

19 Cowan and Easson, 135; Donaldson, 97, 154, 219.

20 *Aberdeen Council Register*, i, 315.

21 Cowan and Easson, 135; *RMS*, v, *no* 618.

22 Fraser, *Green*, 20.

23 Anderson, i, 238.

24 *MS Sasine Register*, i, 206; i, 414, for example.

25 *St Nich Cart*, i, 60.

26 Stones, *Friaries*, 38.

27 *MS Aberdeen Archives*, press 19, bundle 24. Thanks are due to Miss J Cripps for her assistance.

28 *MS Aberdeen Archives*, press 19, bundle 24.

archaeology

waterlogging during the early medieval period, from the Denburn and the Dee, with the gradual development of garden soil layers from the later medieval period onwards.[33]

E *104 Green NJ 940 060*

no archaeological results
Archaeological observation of trenches dug within the standing building revealed only natural levels.[34]

F *2–12 Rennie's Wynd NJ 940 060*

waterlogging in medieval period
This site, shown on Gordon's map of 1661 **figure 6** as garden ground with few buildings, appeared from archaeological observation during redevelopment to have been subject to flooding and waterlogging during much of the medieval period.[35]

notes

29 Stones, *Friaries*, 35–49.

30 Further information from Arts and Recreation Department, Arts and Museums, Art Gallery, Schoolhill, Aberdeen, AB10 1FQ.

31 Stones, *Friaries*, 49–50.

32 Murray, 88–90.

33 *Ibid*, 91–5.

34 *Ibid*, 108.

35 *Ibid*, 108.

area 11

Union Street to Trinity Quay, Market Street to Virginia Street, including Shiprow **figure 34**

historic sites and monuments known from documentary and cartographic sources

St Katherine's Chapel

This chapel stood on St Katherine's Hill (obliterated by construction of Union Street, but visible in the modern lines of Shiprow and Netherkirkgate) and is said to have been built in 1242 by the constable of Aberdeen.[1] This reputation, however, may have resulted from an over-literal interpretation of a comment by the chaplain of St Katherine's, Sir John Cuming, in 1542 that the chapel 'was foundit and biggyit iijc yeir syne be the constabill of Abirdene'.[2] By 1661, according to Gordon's map **figure 6**, the chapel had disappeared.

archaeological potential and future development

The history and development of the harbour area, so fundamental to the growth and prosperity of the burgh and city from medieval times onwards, is extremely complex. Much of the line of the medieval frontage has been infilled and was built over from the seventeenth century onwards. There is, however, the potential for further archaeological work at *Shore Brae* as the time and resources available for previous excavations there were

figure 34
Area 11
© Crown Copyright

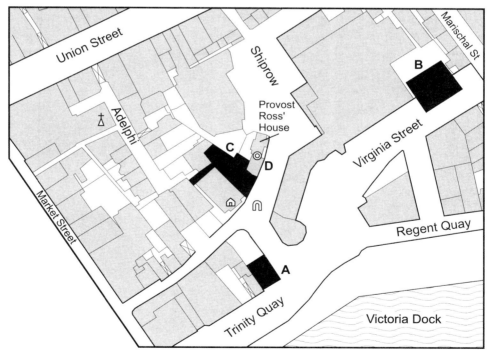

AREA 11

  0   50m

⚲ archaeological excavation

⚲ site of St Katherine's Chapel
🏠 site of 64 Shiprow
🏛 site of Shiprow Port
◎ site of coin hoard

A Shore Brae
B No 3 Bonded Warehouse
C Maritime Museum, Shiprow
D Provost Ross' House coin hoard

80

figure 35
No 64 Shiprow at the
time of its demolition
in 1876

There is no documentary evidence of a nunnery attached to this chapel, as is sometimes claimed. To date there is no archaeological evidence of St Katherine's Chapel.

Shiprow Port

history

This port or gate of entry or exit to the burgh, was probably in existence by the first half of the fifteenth century. Sometimes called the Trinity Port, because of its proximity to the

archaeology

very limited (*see below*). Some pottery-rich medieval and later deposits survived at *no 3 Bonded Warehouse* excavation (*below*); and should any major harbour developments take place in the area to the *south of Virginia Street*, it is possible that further material evidence of the growth of New Aberdeen's shore area could be gained. This area, then, remains a high archaeological priority.

Redevelopment is planned towards the south end of Adelphi. This work will require careful archaeological monitoring, though the evidence from beneath the extension to the *Maritime Museum* suggests that the top portion of St Katherine's Hill has previously been extensively scarped. The discovery of a coin hoard in *Provost Ross' House* is a salutory reminder of the possibility of archaeological evidence being preserved *within* historic standing buildings, as well as beneath them, and of the potential for chance finds.

previous archaeological work and chance finds

A *Shore Brae NJ 943 061*

fourteenth- to fifteenth-century harbour wall
A small-scale excavation at this site, adjacent to the innermost point of Aberdeen's early harbour, indicated the presence of portions of a late 14th/early 15th-century ashlar-faced harbour wall **figure 36**, and traces of subsequent waterfront infill.[9]

figure 36

Fragment of the late fourteenth- to early fifteenth-century harbour wall © Crown Copyright, Historic Scotland

Trinitarian Friary (Area 10), it checked traffic to and from the south side of St Katherine's Hill and from the town's harbour. It may have existed until the eighteenth century. To date there is no archaeological evidence of this structure (*see* pp 11–13 for further information on town defences).

no 64 Shiprow

A little is known of this building from a photograph taken at the time of its demolition in 1876 **figure 35**. Built in 1692, it was typical of a range of three-storeyed buildings with attics which once characterised the major streets in the burgh.[3]

tolbooth

history

According to Gordon there was a tolbooth situated near to the shore, at the west end of present Virginia Street.[4] In the Aberdeen Burgh Court Roll of 1317 this is three times referred to as *tolloneum*—the place where tolls are collected, as opposed to *pretorium*, the

archaeology

B *no 3 Bonded Warehouse, Virginia Street* NJ *944 062*

waterfront area, midden deposits, land reclamation
Gravel and sand layers at this site contained pottery of the late twelfth to fourteenth centuries. The remains of wooden posts associated with these layers may represent traces of mooring posts or jettying, while a group of clench bolts may have been the fragmentary remnants of a boat. Later midden deposits included a wider range of imported pottery than is known from previous Aberdeen sites, perhaps reflecting 'high-status' rubbish from the Castlegate area. Fifteenth- and sixteenth-century garden soil reflected the beginnings of land reclamation in the harbour area. Substantial warehouse and other dockland buildings were constructed in the eighteenth and nineteenth centuries.[10]

C *Maritime Museum, Shiprow* NJ *943061*

no archaeological results
Excavation took place here prior to the construction of the extension to the Aberdeen Maritime Museum. No pre-modern levels remained above the sand subsoil, which demonstrated the great extent to which the south slope of St Katherine's Hill had previously been scarped.

82

later Latin word for the vernacular 'tolbooth'.[5] It may be that there is evidence here of a building which functioned mainly as a collection point for the king's dues,[6] without necessarily the additional, more sophisticated, function of a burgh court assembly room, although it may have served this purpose on occasion.[7] Burgh courts might also be held in a church, private house, or even the open air,[8] although it does appear from the burgh records that from 1398 courts were held regularly in the old tolbooth until their transference to the new.

To date there has been no archaeological evidence of this structure. The excavation at *no* 3 Bonded Warehouse (*see below*) lay a little to the east of the traditional site of the old tolbooth, but it produced no relevant information.

harbour (see below, and also **area 12***)*

historic standing buildings

Provost Ross' House, 48 Shiprow

The eastern section of this house was built *c* 1593; some original features survive, for example an arched fireplace and a stone sink. The western section dates from the early eighteenth century. The first owner may have been John Menzies of Pitfoddels. A 'coin hoard' was found here prior to 1886 (*see below*). The house is now the property of the National Trust for Scotland and houses Aberdeen Maritime Museum.

notes

1	*Aberdeen Description*, 9.	5	*Abdn Recs*, 13, 15 and 17.
2	*Aberdeen Council Register*, i, 181. Thanks are due to Dr Iain Fraser for his views on St Katherine's Chapel. *See also* a full discussion in Fraser, *Thesis*.	6	The king's great customs were collected in the 'scaccarium' in Exchequer Row; Fraser, *Street Names*, 66.
3	Stones, *Two Burghs*, 44.	7	*Abdn Recs*, cxxv.
history 4	*Aberdeen Description*, 9.	8	Robertson, 338–9.

archaeology

D *Provost Ross' House, 48 Shiprow* NJ *943061*

coin hoard

A 'curious collection of old coins and buttons' was found prior to 1886 when a stone had to be removed during repairs in one of the rooms of Provost Ross' House. The majority of the coins were reportedly 'Scottish twopenny pieces of the reign of Charles I'.[11]

notes

9	Murray, J C, 37–45.	11	Evans and Thain, 334.
10	Stones and Cameron (forthcoming).		

area 12

the harbour—area to north and west of Victoria Dock and Albert Basin, including the settlement of Footdee (or Futty) in the east, extending to Market Street in the west and overlapping Areas 8, 9, and 11 in the north-west **figure 37**

historic sites and monuments known from documentary and cartographic sources

the blockhouse

To defend the harbour of Aberdeen a blockhouse or fort was erected on the Sandness in the first half of the sixteenth century, its construction having commenced in 1513–14 prior to the battle of Flodden. It may have replaced an earlier fort dating from 1477.[1] By 1542, the sixteenth-century blockhouse was virtually complete. It was constructed of stone

archaeological potential and future development

No excavations have so far been undertaken in Area 12. Although the potential for survival of archaeological deposits in this area is perhaps low given the scale of redevelopment which has taken place here, any significant ground disturbance should be archaeologically monitored. The chance discovery of at least two medieval coin hoards in this area is of note (*below*). Any surviving archaeological evidence for the sixteenth-century blockhouse would be useful.

previous chance finds

A *Clarence Street NJ 950 061*

medieval coin hoard
Sewer works in Clarence Street, Futty, in August 1867 disturbed a red clay 'jar' containing perhaps up to 1,000 Edwardian (thirteenth- to fourteenth-century) silver pennies. The jar was broken by a workman's pick and most of the coins were scattered in the soil or appropriated by the workmen; their whereabouts now is unknown. Another jar found nearby was empty.[23]

figure 37
Area 12
© Crown Copyright

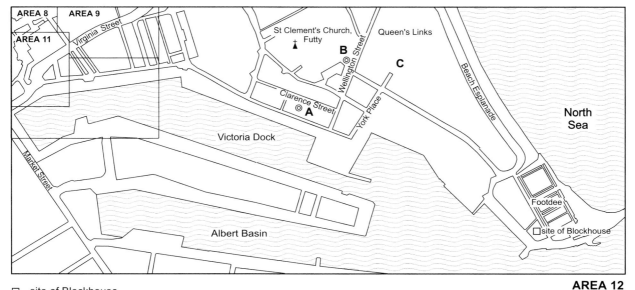

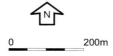

□ site of Blockhouse
◎ approximate site of coin hoard
A Clarence Street coin hoard
B Wellington Street coin hoard
C York Place burials

0   200m

AREA 12

84

and lime, measured 36 ft (10.97 m) by 18 ft (5.49 m), and had walls 6 ft (1.83 m) thick, pierced by gun holes. Instructions in that year that it should be covered with turf indicate that the fort was then still roofless.[2] Across the mouth of the Dee was built a complementary watchtower, which housed a bell to warn of approaching danger. Entrance to the harbour was controlled by a chain which was kept on the surface of the water by masts of ships attached along its length. By 1661, the blockhouse was 'not made use off' bot in the tyme of great alarms and when forrayne incursions are feared'.[3]To date there is no archaeological evidence of this structure.

historic standing buildings

harbour

The natural sheltered harbour at the mouth of the Denburn doubtless served as the haven for the first settlers at Aberdeen. Small boats would be pulled up onto the shelving beach, but it is probable that a man-made quay was constructed early—and certainly before 1399 when there is documentary evidence of 'our key of Abirden'.[4] This appears to have been along the line of Shore Brae[5] and built of ash-wood.[6] By 1413 it was described as an 'open common space'.[7] At some stage, probably in the fifteenth century, the wooden jetty was replaced by a stone and clay construction (*see* Shore Brae, **area 11**). In 1453, £53 was spent on the quay and in 1484 it was either repaired or totally rebuilt, having become ruinous.[8] Deterioration in the state of the quay may have been partially due to the natural silting action prevalent at the mouth of the Denburn. It has been suggested that by the end of the fifteenth century the area sheltered by the quay head was noticeably filling up with silt and refuse,[9] a phenomenon that recurred throughout the next two centuries. In an attempt to curtail this potentially calamitous process the town council enacted in 1561, for example, that any vessel casting out ballast within the flood mark should be subject to a fine of 40 shillings.[10] At the same time as the 1484 repairs, further efforts were made to improve the harbour facilities. Beacons were erected and the wreck of a Spanish ship which obstructed the deeper water channel near the south shore was removed.[11]

The sixteenth century was to witness a series of repair works: in 1512 and 1526 when the master of shorework was sent to Dundee to 'buy famous stones'; in 1549 when further improvements were effected and a stair was added to the quay to facilitate loading and unloading; in 1561 when the costs of some of the repairs were covered by the sale of ornaments and vessels from St Nicholas Church; and in 1582 when a crane was erected.[12] The blockhouse and associated work was aimed at improving the safety of Aberdeen's harbour and a lighthouse set up in St Ninian's Chapel in 1566, which was to burn during the hours of darkness between 1 September and 31 March, facilitated navigation. The building of a wash-house, which was later to serve as a custom house, was one of several additions to the wharf and associated land in the sixteenth century.[13]

history

archaeology

B *Wellington Street* NJ 952 060

?medieval coin hoard
Excavations for a sewer in 1827 in Wellington Street, Futty, produced 'a quantity of gold and silver coins ... sufficient to fill a hat', of uncertain date but possibly English, 'among the first of the Edwards'.[24] The coins were mostly 'carried off by the workmen'. The newspaper account of the discovery of this hoard refers also to an earlier discovery, found perhaps *c* 1806–27, but no further details have come to light.[25]

C *York Place* NJ 954 061

disturbed burials
Excavation to install a new drain in a yard operated by Mobil Oil uncovered

Further improvements were made throughout the seventeenth century. Between 1607 and 1610 a pier was built into the south channel opposite Sandness. Constructed of uncemented stones and loose stakes of timber, its purpose was to force the current of the shallow shore margin onto a channel where it would excavate a deeper passage. A major extension of the wharf on the north shore commenced in 1623 and was completed only thirty-six years later. As a result the area from the quayhead eastwards to the site of the later Regent Quay - the Shorelands - was claimed from the sea.[14] Before 1661 a dock for the repair and building of ships was constructed at Futty.[15]

In spite of all these improvements access to the harbour of Aberdeen still posed difficulties. The great stone, 'Knock Maitland' or 'Craig Metellan' had been removed in 1610,[16] but a bar at the entrance at low water allowed a mere 2 ft (0.61 m) draft of water, exacerbated at times of flood, for example in 1637 when, it is claimed, so much sand, clay and stone were carried down to the sea that 'at low water a man might have passed ... dry footed from the north shore to the bulwark'.[17] By 1661, Gordon portrayed succinctly the disadvantage of Aberdeen's harbour, improved though it was:

> *Men of warre and merchand ships of greatest syze and burthen ly at Torrie*
> *in verie channell of the river Dee. Lesser vessels goe up to Futtie, or by help*
> *of the tyde at high water goe up to the citie, and ly closse all along the peer,*
> *where they ather unload ther goods or take in their fraught.*[18]

The eighteenth-century harbour developments, and in particular the work of Smeaton from the 1770s, were to overcome many of these natural disadvantages, as noted by Douglas on his tour of the east coast. His view of the unimproved harbour was that it was 'long a great detriment to (Aberdeen's) trade, and occasioned the loss of many lives, and much property. A stranger could never depend upon finding it as he left it.'[19]

St Clement's Church and the settlement of Futty or Footdee

The Church of St Clement was reputed to have been erected *c* 1498 to serve the small fishing settlement at Futty. The reference at this date, however, is only to the collection of moneys from the fishers for the 'kirk wark'. The chapel was in existence by at least 22 June 1467 when it was being thatched.[20] After the Reformation the chapel fell into decay until 1631 when an endowment for a clergyman was provided by the townspeople.[21] Attached was a burial ground which was enclosed in 1650 at the expense of George Davidson, Laird of Pettens.[22] The chapel was replaced in 1788. The present building, now redundant, dates from 1828.

The 'town' of Futty, Fittie or Footdee has always been seen as distinct and separate from the adjacent burgh of Aberdeen. In part this reflects its geographical situation, lying on the north bank of the Dee at some distance from the nucleus of Aberdeen, but also its

history

---

archaeology

disarticulated human remains.[26] Portions of a minimum of three individuals were recovered in a beach sand layer some 0.50 m below the tarmac surface of the yard. In 1647 Aberdeen suffered severely from plague and a contemporary reference suggests burial in the sands, while tradition holds that near this spot was one of the main burial areas. These remains were probably disturbed during earlier building work nearby, possibly in 1891, when sewer construction is said to have uncovered a large number of skeletons.[27]

notes

23	Evans and Thain, 328.	26	*Discovery and Excavation in Scotland*
24	*Ibid*, 331.		*1987*, 17.
25	*Ibid*, 330.	27	Milne, 109.

86

origins and the very different way of life led by its inhabitants who were dependent upon fishing for their livelihood.

The earliest inhabitants of Futty probably lived in the vicinity of the church, but harbour developments in the nineteenth century made necessary some re-housing in the 'squares', near the site of the Blockhouse.

St Anne's Hospital, Futty (see **area 14**, *leper hospital)*

notes

1	Meldrum, 21.		11	*Ibid*, 275.
2	*Aberdeen Council Register*, i, 184.		12	*Ibid*, 276; Milne, 361–2.
3	*Aberdeen Description*, 17.		13	Milne, 361–2.
4	*Abdn Recs*, i, 106.		14	*Ibid*, 363.
5	Robertson, 275.		15	Robertson, 280–281.
6	Diverres, A H, 'Britain in Froissart's "Meliador"', in Whitehead, F, Diverres, A H, and Sutcliffe, F G (edd), *Medieval Miscellany presented to Eugene Vinaver*, 100.		16	*Ibid*, 279.
			17	*Ibid*, 281–282.
			18	*Aberdeen Description*, 18.
			19	Douglas, 151.
7	*RMS*, i, 415.		20	*Accounts, Extracts*, v, 23. I am indebted to Dr Iain Fraser for his views on St Clement's Chapel.
8	Robertson, 275.			
9	Murray, J C, 42.		21	Robertson, 255.
10	Robertson, 281.		22	*Ibid*, 257.

history

area 13

area including Union Glen, Hardgate and Justice Mill Brae **figure 38**

historic sites and monuments known from documentary and cartographic sources

Justice Mills

The earliest documentary reference to a mill in this area dates from 1398, and from that date onwards written records provide a useful body of evidence about the industry. The mills had a large catchment area in their heyday, being responsible for grinding the grain brought in from Hazlehead, Kingswells, Newhills, Countesswells and all lands lying to the west of the burgh. The last mill operated well into modern times and was demolished in 1931. It is assumed that the medieval mill may have occupied the same or a closely adjacent site,[1] but archaeological investigation has so far produced no direct evidence of this structure.

archaeological potential and future development

Little is known of the archaeological potential of this area since only one site assessment and no watching briefs have been carried out. However, any future developments within the area of the mill should be subject to archaeological observation and, if necessary, assessment. No sites are currently under threat of development.

previous archaeological work and chance finds

Hardgate / Union Glen NJ 934 056–935 056

nineteenth-century pottery, natural levels
Site evaluation in 1995, prior to redevelopment a little to the east of the site of the Justice Mills, revealed a deep accumulation of garden soil containing nineteenth-century pottery and natural levels.[2]

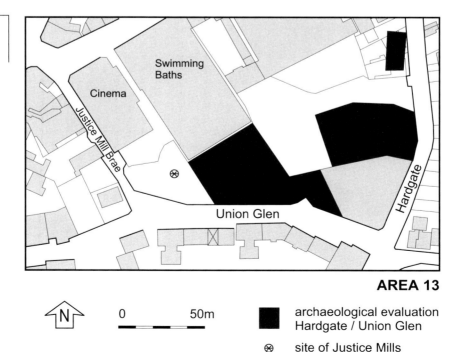

figure 38
Area 13
© Crown Copyright

AREA 13

N 0 50m

■ archaeological evaluation Hardgate / Union Glen

⊗ site of Justice Mills

88

There are no historic standing buildings in Area 13 which fall within the scope of this survey.

note

history   1   *Aberdeen Council Register*, i, 57–104.

archaeology   note

2   Further information from Arts and
     Recreation Department, Arts
     and Museums, Art Gallery,
     Schoolhill, Aberdeen, AB10 1FQ.

area 14
area to the east of King's Crescent and south of St Peter Street **figure 39**

historic sites and monuments known from documentary and cartographic sources

leper hospital

A leper house may have been founded by 1333, when Spitalhill is referred to as *mons hospitalis*, although this name may be derived from St Peter's Hospital which stood on the upper slopes of the hill.[1] By 1363, there is firm documentation for 'the houses of the lepers' which was at the foot of the hill.[2] Such a situation, outwith the town, to ensure isolation of the sick and avoid contamination of the healthy, was the normal practice of many medieval towns. Leper hospitals, however, housed those suffering not only from leprosy but also other skin diseases and, indeed, the sick in general. The leper house is referred to often as the 'the sick house' from 1512 onwards, although described as the *hospitale leprosum* in 1526. This dual appellation has perhaps caused confusion and the belief in a sick house elsewhere, near Futty Port. The leper house(s) and sick house were

archaeological potential and future development

The archaeological priority for Area 14 is to determine the siting, nature and development of the recorded leper hospital. Any developments in the area to the *north of the fire station complex* should be monitored; the transport depot in that location is another possible site for the *leper hospital*.

figure 39
Area 14

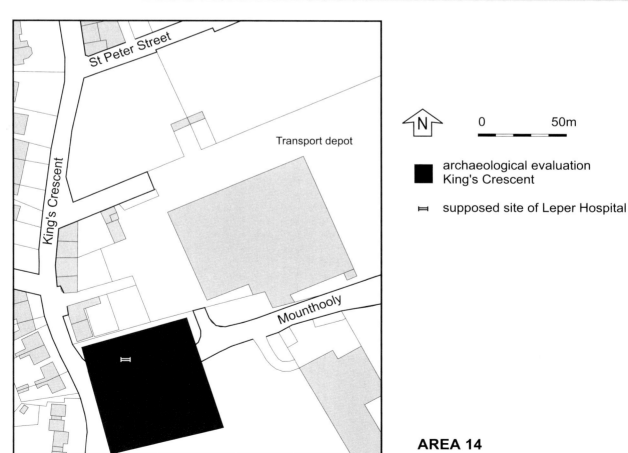

AREA 14

90

identical.[3] In 1574, the council was ordered to collect a rental due on land belonging to the hospital 'betwix New and Auld Aberdeen' and with this to have the leper house repaired and thatched.[4] The house was still in use in 1610 when a leper woman was in residence.[5] By 1661 it was in ruins, and its lands were sold to King's College in 1718.[6]

To date no archaeological evidence of the leper hospital has emerged, though an excavation took place at one supposed site in 1990 (*see* King's Crescent, *below*).

There are no historic standing buildings in Area 14 which fall within the scope of this survey.

notes

history

1   *Abdn Reg*, i, 54.
2   *Ibid*, 54.
3   *MS Aberdeen Council Register*, ix, 156;
       xii, 132, 425; xiv, 197; xv, 705;
       xvi, 602, 704, 873. Thanks
       are due to Dr Iain Fraser for

these references and for his views
on the hospitals of Old and New
Aberdeen; *see also* Fraser, *Thesis*.
4   Cowan and Easson, 168.
5   *Abdn Eccl Rec*, 73–4.
6   Cowan and Easson, 168.

archaeology

previous archaeological work and chance finds

King's Crescent NJ 941 072

leper hospital site
Six trenches were excavated in 1990 ahead of road construction in the supposed area of the leper hospital, first referred to in the mid fourteenth century. A few post-holes may have been medieval features, but the depth of overburden (in excess of 3 m) prohibited further excavation.[7] During 1994–95, the construction of a new road (Mounthooly) and fire station at the site trial-trenched in 1990 was observed by archaeologists, but no relevant features were identified.

note

7   *Discovery and Excavation in Scotland*
       1990, 17.

Old Aberdeen

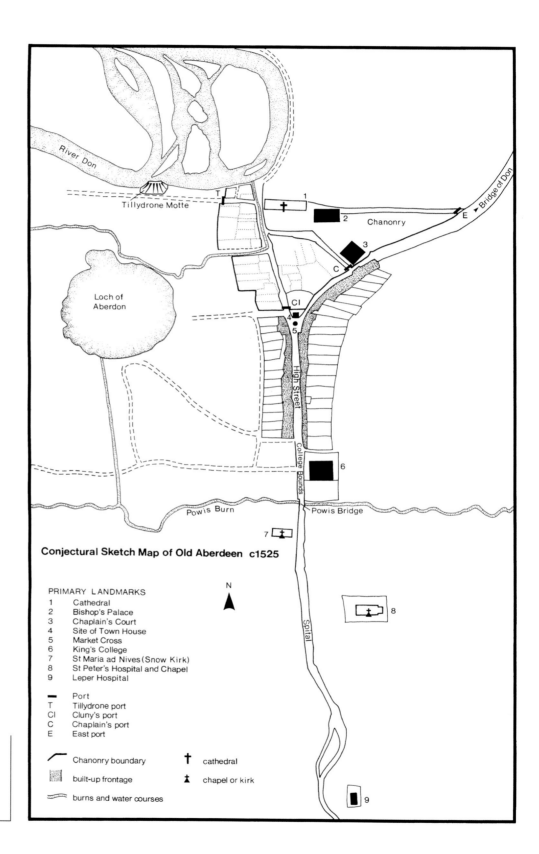

Conjectural Sketch Map of Old Aberdeen c1525

PRIMARY LANDMARKS
1   Cathedral
2   Bishop's Palace
3   Chaplain's Court
4   Site of Town House
5   Market Cross
6   King's College
7   St Maria ad Nives (Snow Kirk)
8   St Peter's Hospital and Chapel
9   Leper Hospital

━   Port
T   Tillydrone port
Cl   Cluny's port
C   Chaplain's port
E   East port

Chanonry boundary   † cathedral
built-up frontage   ⚑ chapel or kirk
burns and water courses

figure 40

A conjectural sketch
map of Old
Aberdeen
c 1525

Old Aberdeen achieved formal status as a burgh of barony on 26 December 1489 as a result of James IV's 'special favour, zeal and affection ... towards William of Elphinstone, Bishop of Aberdeen.'[1] A community, however, had probably been established here beside a church centuries earlier, hence its name 'Old Aberdeen'—to distinguish it from the newer settlement, 'New Aberdeen', to the south. There is a tradition that the first church was one founded beside the River Don by St Machar, reputedly one of the companions of St Columba. The dedication to St Machar certainly suggests early religious associations. At the instance of David I in 1125/1130, a new bishopric was established at Old Aberdeen, probably after transference from Mortlach,[2] and soon after this a church may have been built, or an old church replaced. The establishment of a bishopric and eventually a cathedral chapter created not merely a demand for an ongoing work-force of stone masons, joiners and the like but also the need for the routine services of food-suppliers, 'bakers, brewers, butchers and sellers of flesh and of fish, and other craftsmen'.[3] The route from Old Aberdeen to the trading settlement at New Aberdeen via the Spital ridge and Gallowgate offered a ready access for traders and a natural outlet for their goods from the more northerly settlement. Although small, a viable community was well-established by the time it received formal status as a burgh.

burgh status and the market

Old Aberdeen's current appearance reveals many late medieval and early modern characteristics. One of the most important attributes of a burgh was its function as a market (*see* **area 17**); and although Old Aberdeen was dominated commercially by the entrepôt, New Aberdeen, its own small market played a crucial role in community life.

The charter of James IV gave to the bishop and his successors the constitutional right to appoint burghal officials, and to make burgesses. The burgesses, moreover, were granted the right to hold a weekly market and two annual fairs.[4] The inhabitants of Old Aberdeen were, therefore, legally empowered to gain from all benefits inherent in the basic notion of a burgh.

The market cross stood in its present position at the north end of the High Street in the open area at the present Townhouse (*see* **area 17**). This precinct housed the weekly Monday market,[5] and wooden booths probably lined the street frontages the length of the High Street. The High Street or 'Middle Toun' was thus the commercial centre of the burgh, although the two annual fairs, it seems, 'stood within the chanry and were great ones'.[6]

the extent and layout of the burgh

Behind the houses on the street frontages, long rigs or tofts stretched to the 'back dykes', and beyond those lay the burgesses' common fields. There is no evidence of repletion or infilling in the backlands of tofts, either in documentary sources or in Gordon of Rothiemay's map of 1661. Such a pressure for space was not a problem in Old Aberdeen. The burgh was not large and in 1636 a census of inhabitants reported a population figure of 832 men, women and children.[7] There was probably a further fifty to one hundred personnel at King's College and in consequence a total population of about 900.[8]

King's College (*see* **area 16**), the first buildings of which were commenced in 1500, formed an integral part of Old Aberdeen's community life, although sited at the south end of High Street and to the north of the small settlement at Spital Hill. This location, a somewhat unsuitable, boggy site, was doubtless determined by the availability of open building ground with a street frontage. The founding of a university by Bishop Elphinstone brought not merely increased demand for the supplies and services of the townspeople, but also considerable prestige to the small community.

The most outstanding focal point of the burgh, however, was the cathedral and the chanonry (*see* **area 18**). The church building must have dominated the townscape in the

94

later Middle Ages, although the ecclesiastical complex held itself apart from the small burgh by 'high strong walls and dikes (for defence in troublesome times)'.[9] Within these walls before the Reformation were the manses and gardens of the canons. Property here was of significantly superior quality to the housing of the lay town dwellers; most of the ecclesiastical property possessed slate roofs rather than thatching, whereas there is no evidence of slate being used for houses in the High Street until the early seventeenth century.[10] As in New Aberdeen, the commonest material for the construction of lay town houses was wood. Remains of immediately pre-Reformation property in the chanonry, however, suggest fine buildings of stone and lime, with well-dressed sandstone being brought from distant quarries.[11]

the Reformation and later

Old Aberdeen's status as a burgh of barony dependent on a bishop was to be shaken by the Reformation. Not only were the cathedral and chanonry to suffer material deprivation but the town also felt itself impoverished financially and culturally.[12] There are indications, however, that the townspeople made efforts to maintain the fabric of their burgh. Improvements were made to private property, and in 1634 the town council enacted that all were to pave in front of their buildings within six weeks or suffer a £10 fine.[13] A census taken two years later gives an insight into the make-up of the town. There was a population of 831 in 202 households. The resultant mean household size—4.11—is an indication of the relatively large number of households with single or widowed men or women at the head. Traditionally, a large number of widows was attracted to the burgh by the relatively generous poor relief of Old Aberdeen, which in the seventeenth century included quarterly pensions. Interestingly, also, the sixty-three male and ninety-six female servants (19.9 per cent of the population) in eighty-seven households highlights the low wages and availability of servants in a poor region, and the number of relatively wealthy lairds, gentlemen and members of the professions still resident in Old Aberdeen.[14] Political events of the seventeenth century were, moreover, to take their toll. By the turn of the century the cathedral was to show further signs of decay: the great tower had fallen in ruins to join those of the bishop's palace. But stone was a valuable, re-usable commodity: the decaying manses were converted and refurbished for lay use or their sites utilised, for example, for a Trades Hospital. In 1725 the stones from the Dunbar Aisle were used to 'help build anew the south side of the college' along with other repairs. A new tolbooth and school were built early in the century; and remedial work was done on the parish church and manse.[15]

Old Aberdeen was to remain a small, close-knit community, perhaps not rising above a population of 1,100 in the eighteenth century. In 1788 it was noted that the burgh still suffered from the old hazard of fires which, it was claimed, were caused by 'the improper manner of cleaning chimneys and from thatched roofs';[16] and Pennant was to describe it in 1769 as 'a poor toon'.[17]

In 1891 the burgh, along with Torry, was assimilated into the city of Aberdeen. Old Aberdeen had not received the twin benefits and disadvantages of major industrialisation; and consequently was to retain much of its intrinsic appeal. In spite of the severing of the northern part of the burgh by a modern thoroughfare, much has survived into the twentieth century. This must be accredited not only to an enlightened official policy of preservation, but also to the support of the friends of those two early dominant influences on the burgh - the cathedral and the university.

notes

1   *Old Abdn Recs*, i, 6–7.

2   Cowan, 2.

3   *Old Abdn Recs*, i, 9.

4   *Ibid*, 8.

5   The market was changed to a Thursday, but, since the burgesses of New Aberdeen complained that a market on this

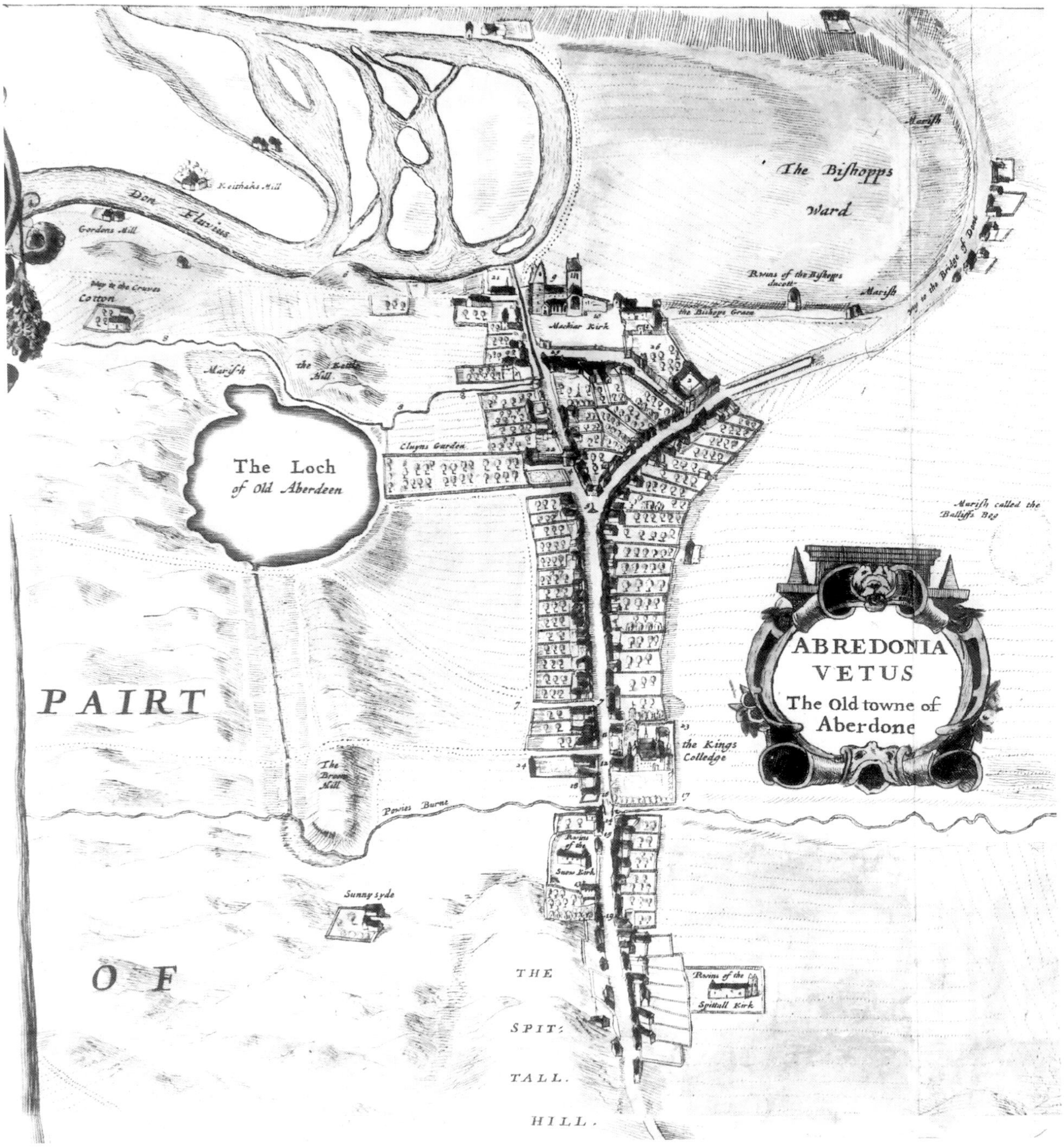
The Bishopps Ward
Don Fluvius
Gordons Mill
Cotton
Machar Kirk
Marish
The Loch of Old Aberdeen
Clunys Garden
PAIRT
OF
ABREDONIA VETUS The Old towne of Aberdone
the Kings Colledge
Powis Burne
Sunny syde
THE SPIT: TALL. HILL.
Spittall Kirk

figure 41
Old Aberdeen, Gordon of Rothiemay's map 1661

day in Old Aberdeen forestalled their market, it was altered to a Tuesday (Milne, 18).

6 Orem, 194.

7 *MS Old Aberdeen Town Council Minutes*, ii, 3–11.

8 Simpson, *Old Aberdeen*, 5.

9 Orem, 79.

10 *Ibid*, 127.

11 Milne, 16.

12 *Ibid*, 19. A petition from the magistrates of Old Aberdeen to the effect that they had been impoverished by the Reformation resulted in the temporary return of the Commissary Court from New Aberdeen to Old Aberdeen.

13 Orem, 154.

14 Tyson, R, 'Household size and structure in a Scottish burgh: Old Aberdeen in 1636', *Local Population Studies*, *no* 40 (1988), 47, 49, 51.

15 Short, *Old Aberdeen*, 5–7.

16 *Old Abdn Recs*; i, 202.

17 Pennant, 116.

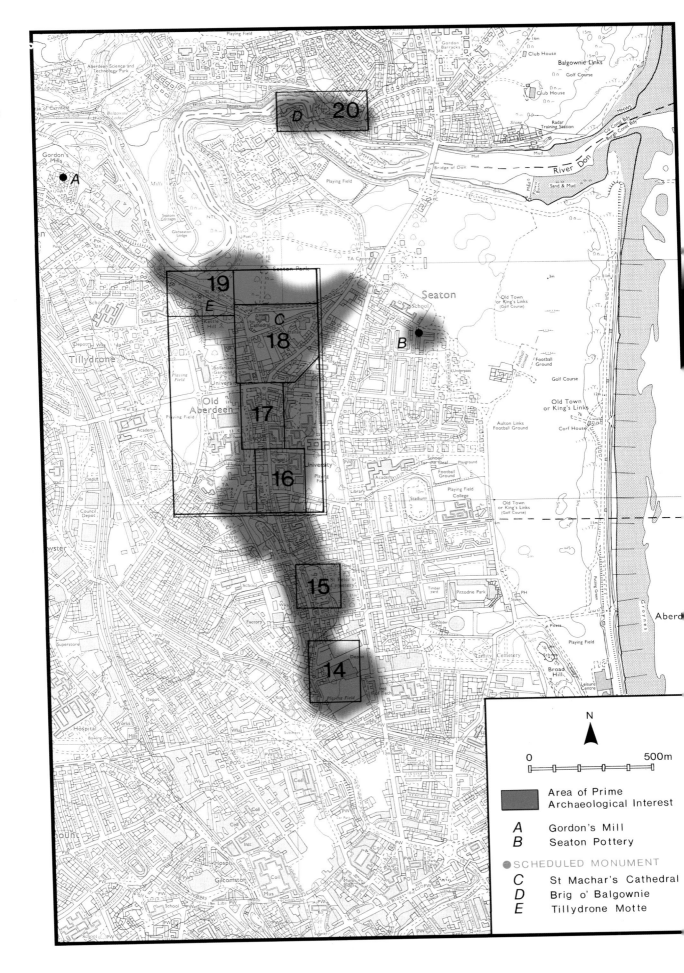

N

0 _____ 500m

Area of Prime
Archaeological Interest

A Gordon's Mill
B Seaton Pottery

●SCHEDULED MONUMENT

C St Machar's Cathedral
D Brig o' Balgownie
E Tillydrone Motte

the archaeology of Old Aberdeen

The position of Old Aberdeen as a Conservation Area, and therefore subject to relatively little large-scale development, has meant that very few archaeological excavations have taken place there. Recent years have brought more opportunities for investigation, but so far little evidence has been found to survive in those areas which have become available for excavation. In one case (*nos* 64–72 Don Street), this lack is attributable to the very shallow topsoil and the destruction of any underlying stratigraphy by intensive market gardening in the nineteenth and twentieth centuries. At the only other substantial excavation site in Old Aberdeen (*no* 81 High Street), some archaeological stratigraphy was intact, though only seventeenth-century and later material was recorded. So far, there has been no location in Old Aberdeen where significant quantities even of medieval pottery have been recovered.

Old Aberdeen is, therefore, relatively under-investigated archaeologically and its archaeological potential remains largely an unknown quantity. Nevertheless, it is one of Scotland's most unaltered historic burghs and the survival of important archaeological deposits is likely in some parts of the burgh, even sometimes in isolated pockets. Any opportunities for excavation and archaeological observation should be taken, in particular at any location in the Chanonry, High Street, or King's College area, with the emphasis on street frontage sites. It is worth recalling here that historic standing buildings may also preserve archaeological evidence both within and beneath their structures, and it is expected that any renovation works will routinely require archaeological monitoring.

98

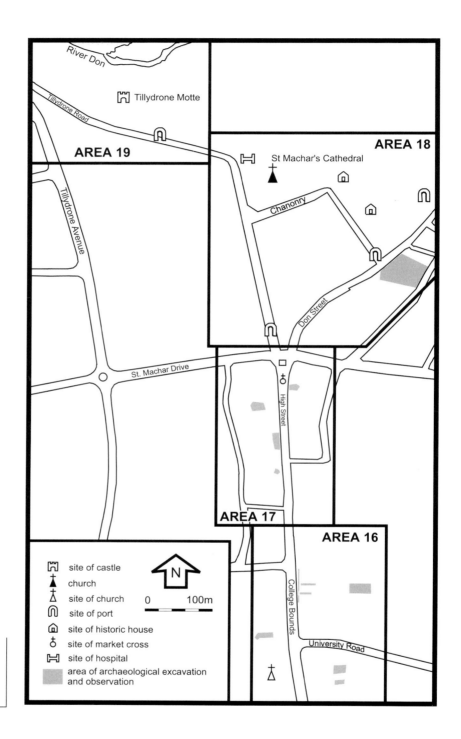

figure 43
Old Aberdeen:
area location map
© Crown Copyright

introduction

For this survey, the core of Old Aberdeen and certain key locations in its immediate vicinity have been placed within six discrete areas (*see* **figures 42** *&* **43**). In order to avoid confusion between areas of New and Old Aberdeen, the areas of the two burghs are numbered consecutively (Areas 1 to 14 are in New Aberdeen; Areas 15 to 20 are in Old Aberdeen). The divisions into areas have been made for the sake of convenience and are not intended to reflect the development of the medieval or later settlement.

area 15
between Spital and St Peter's Cemetery **figure 44**

historic sites and monuments known from documentary and cartographic sources

A *St Peter's Hospital and Chapel*

St Peter's Hospital was founded by Bishop Matthew Kininmund (1172–99) to sustain 'infirm brethren'.[1] A reference to the 'sisters living therein' in 1256 suggests that in due

archaeological potential and future development

No archaeological excavations have been conducted in Area 15 and, though the locations of the *hospital, chapel and burial ground* are known, archaeological investigation could yield information about their layout, extent, organisation and everyday life. Any developments within the *Spital area* in the future will require at least a minimum response of archaeological observation. Clarification of the extent to which the area of the Spital has been scarped since the seventeenth century would be useful (*see 65 Spital, below*).

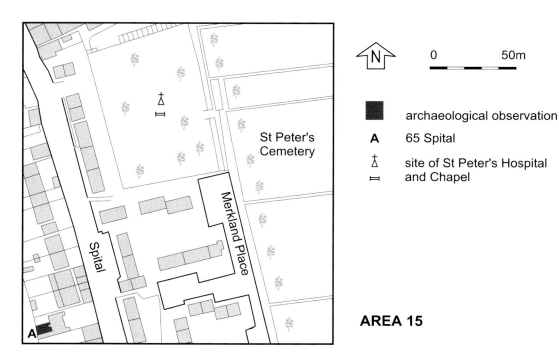

St Peter's Cemetery

Merkland Place

Spital

N

0   50m

■   archaeological observation

A   65 Spital

site of St Peter's Hospital and Chapel

AREA 15

figure 44
Area 15
© Crown Copyright

course women also were maintained.[2] It stood to the east side of the street, the Spital, which takes its name from the hospital, and consisted also of a chapel and a burial ground. This latter was the nucleus of the present St Peter's Cemetery, where the outline of the chapel can still be seen.

The hospital is next recorded in 1427 when Bishop Henry Lichton learnt that the revenues of the hospital were being appropriated by the masters to their own use and to the neglect of the poor.[3] In consequence most of the hospital revenues were diverted to the foundation and support of two chaplainries in the cathedral, although some endowments were retained by the hospital. The sick were still being cared for at St Peter's in 1541.[4] (*See also* entry for *St Maria ad Nives*, **Area 16**, *below*.)

The fragment of St Peter's Chapel is the only physical relic of the historic buildings which once stood in Area 15.

notes

history

1	*Abdn Reg*, i, 11.		3	*Ibid*, ii, 226–7.
2	*Ibid*, ii, 39.		4	Cowan and Easson, 169.

archaeology

previous archaeological work and chance finds

no 65 Spital NJ 940 075

garden/subsoil levels
During construction of an extension to the rear of this property, eighteenth- to nineteenth-century finds were revealed in a garden soil layer overlying natural subsoil. This suggests that the area called 'The Spitall Hill' on Parson Gordon's map of 1661 had been scarped to provide a firm footing for the building.[5]

note

5   *Discovery and Excavation in Scotland
       1994*, 22.

area 16
north end of Spital, College Bounds

historic sites and monuments known from documentary and cartographic sources

St Maria ad Nives (Snow Kirk)

The establishment of *St Maria ad Nives* or St Mary of the Snows was part of William Elphinstone's overall scheme for the founding of a burgh and a university beside the Cathedral of St Machar (*see* pp 112–14). Early in 1498, James IV authorised a supplication to the Pope requesting a restructuring of the parish boundaries of Kirkton of Seaton, the cathedral parish, and also the erection of a new parish of Old Aberdeen which would exclude the chanonry and cathedral, but include the market settlement, the area where Elphinstone was to establish the university, and the Spital region. This request was granted in February; in August James IV confirmed his charter of 1489 which had set up the burgh of Old Aberdeen, but this time, significantly, included the university in all the rights and privileges formerly granted to the burgh alone; and on 10 December Elphinstone erected the new parish.[1]

There were a number of reasons for the establishment of a new parish. Elphinstone was aware that the foundation of the university would mean a considerable influx of people to the new burgh. He did not wish his collegiate church to function as a parish church to this enlarged group. By this new foundation he would be able to separate the cathedral precincts from the new parish, and draw away from the cathedral all its new parishioners, thereby sparing the need to provide an extra vicar to the dean (who was the rector and prebendary of Kirkton, the cathedral parish). Thus, the new parish was founded without interfering with the college routine, or requiring a vicar at the dean's expense, but the new burgh was served and the parishioners of this new parish could receive all the sacraments from their own vicar living in their midst.[2]

archaeological potential and future development

No archaeological excavations have been conducted in Area 16 to date and the only archaeological watching brief to have produced any archaeological information was that undertaken during installation of the King's College floodlighting scheme. Nevertheless, King's College is an ancient and highly significant institution in the history of Old Aberdeen and any further developments in or around the present King's College buildings should be subject to archaeological examination, as should any proposed ground disturbance in the vicinity of St Maria ad Nives (Snow Kirk).

previous archaeological work and chance finds

A *King's College floodlighting* NJ 939 081

drainage channel and cobbled area
Several small trenches were opened up by contractors during the installation of floodlights on the west front of the College. The foundations of the 1832 frontage were exposed. A drainage channel was discovered running parallel to this frontage and was thought to be associated with its construction. At the front of the site, near College Bounds, was a cobbled area, probably of fairly recent date.[17]

B *King's College Conference Centre* NJ 940 081

no archaeological results
Observation during conversion from University Library to Visitor and Conference Centre provided no archaeological evidence.[18]

Equally important perhaps was that Elphinstone, as revealed in the phrase in the foundation charter, *a primeva eius erectione vacante*, was in fact reorganising an existing parish which not only gave a solution to the anomalous position of St Peter's Hospital which had been partially suppressed as a parish in 1427, but also brought the hospital and its parishioners or inmates into the new parish. Elphinstone could legitimately re-appropriate the remaining parochial revenues which had belonged to the hospital, but were now surplus to its needs.[3]

The new parish did not yet have a church. The first reference to its title occurs in 1503,[4] and it was probably about this time that the building of *St Maria ad Nives* was completed. The small church housed two bells brought from the south-west tower of the cathedral[5] and was surrounded by a graveyard. It is clearly visible on Gordon's map of 1661 and remains as a cemetery today.

Soon after the Reformation, a decision was taken that St Machar's should become the sole parish church of Old Aberdeen, although it did not effectively function as such immediately. The Snow Church had, however, outlived its usefulness and in 1583 James declared that 'because the kirks of Machar, Snaw and Spittal were united to the College and University of Aberdeen' and the revenues of the last two were insufficient to appoint a minister, they were to be 'united to the parish and parish church of Machar called the Cathedral Kirk of Aberdeen'.[6]

historic standing buildings

King's College

On 10 February 1495, a college dedicated to St Mary in the Nativity was founded by papal bull at Old Aberdeen, a spot endowed with a 'temperate climate, abundance of victuals, convenience of dwellings and good store of the other things pertaining to human life'.[7] The first students of what was to become named King's College were taught in the manses of the chanonry from 1495, since nearly ten years were to elapse before sufficient funds were available to guarantee the necessary stipends and bursaries, although the building programme of Elphinstone's university was under way almost immediately. The curriculum embraced theology, civil law, canon law, medicine and the liberal arts, and was modelled on the universities of Orleans and Paris. The intention, moreover, was that bursaried students should come from the north-eastern region as a whole, but that poor, gifted candidates should be given priority.[8]

history

archaeology

C *Music Department building NJ 939 080*

no archaeological results
Observation of a small development beside the Music Department of Aberdeen University provided no archaeological results.

D *&* **E** *40–42 and 32 College Bounds NJ 939 080*

natural levels
During demolition, the natural subsoil was exposed directly beneath the modern demolition level.[19]

notes

17–18 Further information from Arts and Recreation Department, Arts and Museums, Art Gallery, Schoolhill, Aberdeen, AB10 1FQ.

19   Murray, J C, 112.

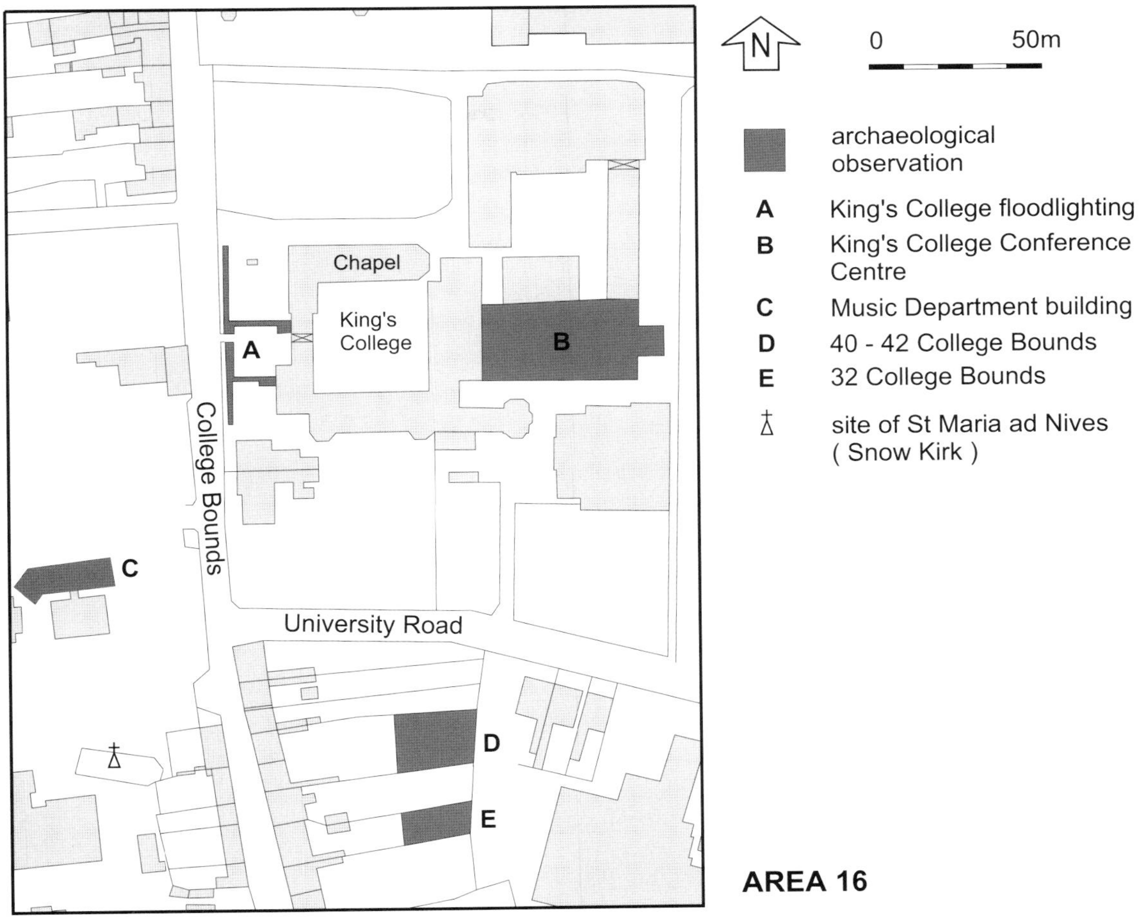

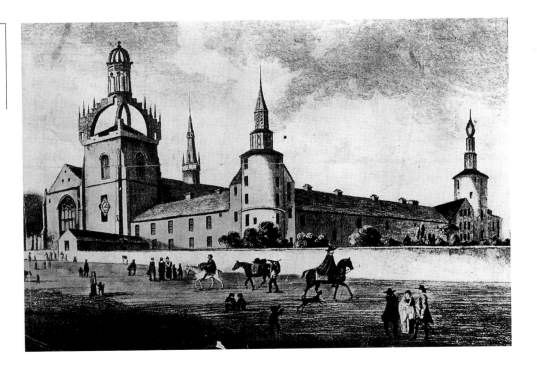

Chapel
King's College
A
B
C
D
E
College Bounds
University Road
N
0
50m
archaeological observation
A King's College floodlighting
B King's College Conference Centre
C Music Department building
D 40 - 42 College Bounds
E 32 College Bounds
site of St Maria ad Nives (Snow Kirk)
AREA 16

figure 45
Area 16
© Crown Copyright

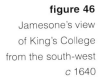

figure 46
Jamesone's view of King's College from the south-west *c* 1640

The nucleus of the university buildings was the quadrangle, which in 1505 was bounded to the north by the chapel and the great hall; to the east by accommodation for the principal and some staff and students, and by the Crown Tower, an open imperial crown, perhaps to assert the Scottish monarchy's imperial pretensions;[9] and to the west and south by chambers for the masters and students. In the centre of the quadrangle stood a well. To the south-west and north-east stood two towers. The latter, the Ivy Tower or Round Tower, completed in 1525 and originally topped with a wooden spire, may have served the university in the repulse of the reforming mob that moved on Old Aberdeen in 1560. It may also have functioned as the repository for the college armoury and precious manuscripts.[10]

To the north of the quadrangle stood the college chapel. In 1498 work had begun on clearing the site, which proved so marshy that foundations had to be laid on rafts of oak. (The falling away to the east of the windows may be evidence of subsidence of the foundations at the north-eastern end during construction). Work on the building, however, was officially begun by 2 April 1500, as is indicated on the original inscription at the north side of the west door of the chapel. Construction was completed by *c* 1504: the date and the royal arms are sculpted on the three central buttresses. The master-mason may have been either Alexander Gray, who had been working on the tower of St Giles Church, Edinburgh, or John Gray, the mason responsible for the nave in St Nicholas Church, New Aberdeen (*see* **area 7**, *above*). The leading of the roof was executed by John Burnel, Henry VII's master-plumber, in 1506.[11] Much of the chapel has survived, in spite of damage at the Reformation: the sixteenth-century oak screen, a rare example of medieval workmanship; the choir stalls which reveal Flemish influence but were perhaps made locally by master joiners including John Fendour;[12] windows with looped and pointed arches and broad central mullions; the 1505 slender spire that bisects the line of the roof; and an early single-faced sundial on the south side of the chapel. Within the quad along the south wall of the chapel there was originally a sacristy, library and jewel house which was completed sometime between 1532 and 1545.

The entire complex was enclosed by a precinct wall, both to isolate students and encourage undistracted study, and possibly for protection. Some buildings and associated lands, however, stood outwith the wall: a manse for the mediciner, for example, stood to the west side of College Bounds,[13] and it was intended to expand still further beyond the Powis Burn.[14]

King's College also suffered mixed fortunes in this period. The purge of Catholic teaching staff in 1569, together with the dismissal of the chapel's eight prebendaries and six choir boys, did not bring a quick regeneration: the New Foundation of 1583, which redesigned the arts course along Melvillian lines, was accompanied by wholesale cuts in the teaching establishment; and in the early years of the seventeenth century most of the chapel windows were broken or built up. Natural disaster also intervened: a storm in 1633 blew down the crown above the chapel. The period of Bishop Patrick Forbes (1618–35) saw further reform, an intellectual revival, the establishment of a printing press and a modest increase in student numbers. But his death cut short his reform programme, and instability and uncertainty were soon to follow in the Covenanting years; the college would take a long period to recover from it. A plan, which had probably originated with Forbes, to unite King's College and Marischal College, founded in 1593 in New Aberdeen, under the title of 'King Charles's University', foundered in 1641. Both colleges refused to cooperate and King's College retained its independence until 1860, when it was united with Marischal College to form an enlarged university. Some reforms, however, were effected during the period of Cromwell's Protectorate and in 1658–62 the 70 ft (21.34 m) high Cromwell Tower was constructed at the east end of the chapel to accommodate extra students on six floors, with four rooms to a floor. This was altered to four floors in the 1820s.[15]

A grammar school (visible on Slezer's vignette **figure 47**) was built between the west facade of the college and College Bounds. This stood until the late eighteenth century when it was removed along with much of the west front. At some date between 1825 and

Facies Civitatis ABERDONIÆ Veteris. The Prospect of OLD ABERDIEN.

figure 47

Vignette from John Slezer's prospect of Old Aberdeen
c 1693

1832 John Smith's west range replaced the south-west tower and the original western facade, apart from the Crown Tower. The southern wing had been replaced in 1730 and was rebuilt again in 1860. The sacristy, jewel house and library had also been rebuilt and enlarged in 1725, and then were destroyed by fire in *c* 1772. The university books were saved, however, and the nave of the chapel served as the library until the new library by Robert Matheson replaced the sixteenth-century east wing.[16]

Four episodes of archaeological watching brief have been carried out in the vicinity of King's College (*see below*), but so far no archaeological evidence relevant to any of the above structures has been recorded.

notes

1   Macfarlane, *Elphinstone*, 134.
2   Thanks are due to Dr L Macfarlane for discussing his views on the motives of Elphinstone in setting up this new parish.
3   Macfarlane, *Elphinstone*, 315.
4   *Ibid*, 315.
5   *Aberdeen Fasti*, 47.
6   *Ibid*, 131–2.
7   *Ibid*, 3–5.
8   *Ibid*, 1–80.
9   The original was blown down in 1633, but replaced with a close copy.
10   Macfarlane, *King's College*, 22.
11   *Ibid*, 3.
12   *Ibid*, 3.
13   *Aberdeen Fasti*, 77.
14   *Ibid*, 80–108.
15   Stevenson, *King's College, Aberdeen, 1560–1641: From Protestant Reformation to Covenanting Revolution*, 41–51, 61–93, 122–3; Brogden, 87.
16   Brogden, 87.

area 17
High Street

historic standing buildings and documentary sources

market cross

The High street or 'Middle Toun' was the commercial centre of the burgh, although the two annual fairs, it seems, 'stood within the chanry and were great ones'.[1] The town's market was held in the open area at the top of High Street and it was here that the market cross was sited. Since the cross bore the arms of Bishops Dunbar, Smart and, in particular, Gordon, it could not have been of earlier date than 1545. It also carried on its north and south sides representations of the Virgin Mary, which were defaced at the Reformation.[2] The remains of the cross now stand in the High Street outside the Town House, a little to the north of the supposed traditional site.

In 1723 a flesh market with a tile roof, as opposed to an open-air structure, was constructed.[3]

---

archaeological potential and future development

Despite the limited opportunities for archaeological investigation which have so far presented themselves in this area, the results have been interesting. Excavation at *81 High Street* suggested that there may have been no pre seventeenth-century occupation on this site; and, just south of here at *59 High Street*, natural levels were encountered immediately beneath the modern. This may suggest that the nucleus of the late medieval burgh was confined to the northern part of the High Street—near the tolbooth and market cross, both of which were essential features of the medieval and later townscape. The possibility of recovering important single finds, such as the grave slab found at *101 High Street*, is always present in this context. Any *developments on or near to the High Street*, including ground disturbance within some standing structures, will continue to require careful archaeological monitoring, and archaeological deposits can be particularly expected towards the northern end of the High Street. No sites are currently known to be under threat of development.

previous archaeological work and chance finds

A *rear of 101 High Street* NJ *938 084*

well, broken grave slab
A well was uncovered during the construction of an extension to the Geography Department of Aberdeen University. The upper two or three courses were built of red brick but the lower courses were drystone. A broken grave slab (now in the care of the City of Aberdeen Arts and Recreation Department, Art and Museums) was found in the well. The inscription read:

> HEER LYES T ...
> OE HENRY KIL ...
> BVRGES IN ABD-DE ...
> OCTOBER.1660 HIS AGE 96
> AND ELIZABETH ANDER
> ... ON ... SPOVS WHO
> ...1659.[5]

tolbooth

Facing down the High Street is Old Aberdeen Town House, a Georgian building made to a design of George Jaffray in 1788. It incorporates to some extent an earlier town house built in 1721. The first tolbooth on this site was constructed in 1702 and functioned as both town council room and gaol. Previously, from 1642, the council had met in the east upper portion of a building erected on the site of the bishop's dovecot, the west upper room functioning as a school room and the lower rooms as weight and meal houses. Before this was constructed, the magistrates convened in the session house of St Machar's Church.[4]

notes

history

1	Orem, 194.	3	*Ibid*, 192.
2	*Ibid*, 187–88.	4	*Ibid*, 189–90.

archaeology

B *104 High Street NJ 939 084*

natural subsoil
Observation during development revealed that the modern levels lay directly on the natural subsoil.[6]

C *81 High Street NJ 939 083*

post-medieval occupation
A frontage site, which had been a garden for many years, on the west side of High Street, was subject to a limited exploratory excavation. The area nearest the frontage had been disturbed by a modern deep sewer trench, but evidence of a cobbled yard dating to the seventeenth century was recovered. There were no indications that this area had been developed prior to that date.[7]

D *59 High Street NJ 939083*

natural levels
Archaeological observation during shop refurbishment indicated natural sand levels beneath the modern ground level.[8]

notes

5	Murray, J C, 110.	8	*Discovery and Excavation in Scotland 1994*, 22.
6	*Ibid*, 112.		
7	Cameron, Johnston and Stones (forthcoming).		

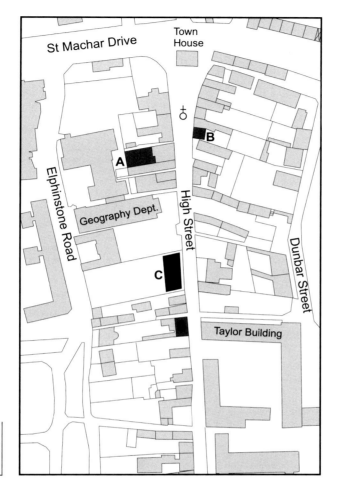

N   0   50m

■ archaeological
   excavation

▨ archaeological
   observation

A   rear of 101 High Street
B   104 High Street
C   81 High Street
D   59 High Street

⚥ site of Market Cross

AREA 17

area 18
St Machar's Cathedral and Chanonry **figure 49**

historic sites and monuments known from documentary and cartographic sources

the cathedral

It is generally accepted that the see which eventually became that of Aberdeen was originally based at the Celtic ecclesiastical centre of Mortlach, and that its transference to Old Aberdeen was effected *c* 1130. Whether there was an already existing church on the site is uncertain, but tradition suggests that this was so. Probably soon after the establishment of the bishopric on this site a new church was built, and around 1157 Bishop Edward received authority from the papacy to provide the cathedral with a chapter of monks or canons. This authorisation, however, seems not to have been implemented immediately, and it was only in the thirteenth century that capitular status was largely achieved.[1]

the chanonry

The chanonry developed around the cathedral. This walled precinct housed the various properties of the canons and other clerics attached to the cathedral. Lining the roadway now called the Chanonry, the pathway leading towards Tillydrone, and that to the south of the cathedral, were the manses of the cathedral canons. The layout of these properties is still discernible. No surface remnants now survive of the bishop's palace, which was situated to the east of the cathedral. A modern university residence, Dunbar Hall, now occupies the site. The palace was 'a large court having four towers, one in every corner of the close and a great hall and chambers'.[2] In the centre of the courtyard was a well and to the south-east was a garden. On the south side of the court were outer and inner ports. Access could also be gained by the water gate to the north which led to the Don, or by a passage through an iron gate which led directly to the chancel and thus to the church. The Bishop's Port (NJ 9413 0876) was erected *c* 1429; the Chaplain's Port (NJ 9405 0864) was erected *c* 1532 and stood until at least 1725; and Cluny's Port stood until the close of the eighteenth century. No trace remains of any of these ports, or of the wall itself.

archaeological potential and future development

No watching briefs have taken place in Area 18 and no chance finds have been reported. The only archaeological work to have taken place in this area so far proved disappointing (*64–72 Don Street*). This site was, however, some 150 m to the south-east of the *cathedral and chanonry* where archaeological remains, including evidence for the bishop's palace and related structures, could be particularly expected; nor is it by any means proven that the whole of the *Don Street frontage* has been disturbed by modern horticulture. Any archaeological evidence for the three known port sites should also be sought. Given the relative lack of archaeological observations and investigations to date, any developments within this area will require careful monitoring in the future, including any involving ground disturbance within standing buildings. No sites are known currently to be facing development threats.

previous archaeological work and chance finds

nos 64–72 Don Street NJ 940 086

eighteenth- to twentieth-century wells, buildings, furnaces
What should have been a promising frontage site, east of the main road to the north from

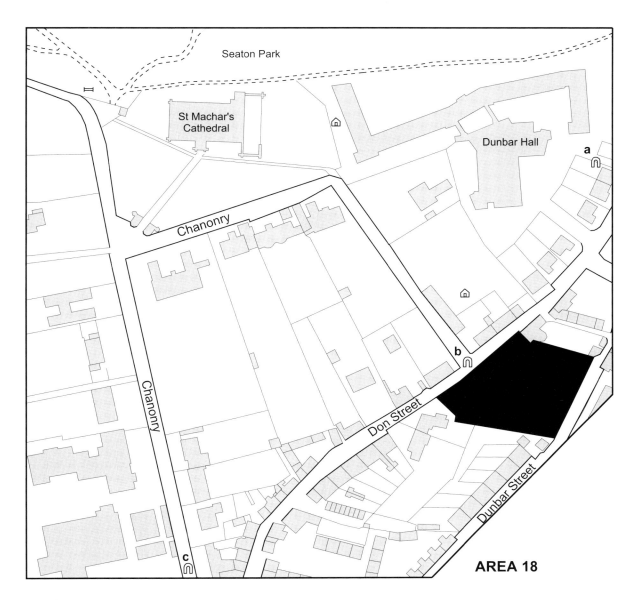

Seaton Park

St Machar's
Cathedral

Dunbar Hall

a

Chanonry

Chanonry

Don Street

Dunbar Street

b

c

AREA 18

N

0   50m

archaeological excavation
64-72 Don Street

site of port
  a East Port
  b Chaplain's Port
  c Cluny's Port

site of historic house
  d Chaplain's Chambers
  e Bishop's Palace

site of Bishop's Hospital

figure 49
Area 18
© Crown Copyright

school

A school was attached to the cathedral in the Middle Ages for the education, particularly in music and song, of boys training to be choristers.

historic standing buildings

the Cathedral of St Machar and the chanonry

the pre-Reformation cathedral
According to Boece, the building of the first cathedral was begun before the death of King Malcolm IV (1165),[3] which is partially confirmed by the only surviving remnant of this early cathedral—an abacus of a small Romanesque pillar. During the episcopate of Henry Cheyne (1282–1328) there was some demolition of this early cathedral (although it may have been only the choir and apse that was affected),[4] in order to erect a larger edifice, suitable to accommodate the cathedral chapter that had evolved: the canons and four dignitaries of the cathedral, as well as lesser clerics and choir boys. There appears to be only one survivor of Bishop Cheyne's choir; a corbel forming part of the inside arch of a large gothic window.[5]

Succeeding bishops were to devote much of their energy and wealth to the extension and beautifying of the cathedral. Bishop Alexander Kininmund (1355–80) began the construction of what was probably intended to be a cruciform church similar to those of Elgin and St Andrews. At the eastern end of the present nave can be seen the fine sandstone western piers of the bell-tower constructed at this time. The task of completing the nave, however, fell to Bishop Henry Lichton (1422–40). This was achieved in granite, which affords a certain magnificence to the building, but reveals a lack of finesse and detail, particularly at the junction with Kininmund's crossing and where the twin westerly towers encroach on the pre-existing bay design of the aisles. In consequence the aisles were covered by a wooden lean-to roof.[6] Bishop Lindsay (1441–58) was responsible for roofing the nave with slates and paving the floor; and his successor, Thomas Speirs (1458–80), completed the glazing of the windows and added luxurious trappings to the interior.

A culmination of this work was largely achieved by the episcopate of William Elphinstone (1483–1514). He took firm measures to improve the service of the clergy of his diocese and of the chapter, and reformed the liturgy, which resulted in the production of the Aberdeen Breviary.[7] He also did much to perfect the fabric of the cathedral. By 1511, he had completed Henry de Lichton's chancel with the addition of a belfry and spire to the central tower. The work had been undertaken by John Fendour, perhaps to a design of Elphinstone's with the assistance of Canon Alexander Galloway, Rector of Kinkell. The timber spire was covered in lead, as was to be that of St Nicholas Parish

history

archaeology | Old Aberdeen and just outside the Chaplain's port, proved to have been seriously disturbed by horticulture in the nineteenth and early twentieth centuries. Only features cut into the natural sand remained. Two eighteenth-century stone-lined wells were discovered, one associated with buildings of that date along the Don Street frontage, and one towards the rear of the site. In addition, the bases of two brick-built peat-fired furnaces and a fire-pit, probably eighteenth-century in date, were found near the Don Street frontage. All traces of superstructure had disappeared. A single ditch ran approximately west to east across part of the site, and may have been a boundary of sixteenth- to seventeenth-century date.[18]

note

18   Cameron, Johnston and Stones (forthcoming).

Church, New Aberdeen. The slate and stone roofs of St Machar's were likewise replaced
with lead.[8]

Elphinstone's building projects remained uncompleted by his death; but these and his
ecclesiastical reforms were taken up by his successor, Gavin Dunbar (1518–32). Dunbar is
perhaps best remembered for the addition to the nave of a unique heraldic ceiling,
portraying the political situation of Scotland and Christendom in the early sixteenth
century.[9]

Other additions and alterations were made: the cap-house roofs on the twin west
towers were replaced with spires of sandstone, to counterbalance the new central steeple;
and the south transept, where Dunbar is buried, was remodelled and completed. It would
seem, however, that at his death the new choir was still incomplete,[10] and was to remain so
throughout the episcopate of his successor, William Stewart (1532–45). The building
programme was never to reach its conclusion, and much that had been achieved was to be
destroyed or allowed to fall to waste during and after the Reformation.

post-Reformation history

The building and furnishings of St Machar's were to suffer sadly as a result of the
Protestant Reformation. In January 1560, a mob from Angus and the Mearns, having
failed to purge King's College of popery, moved on to the chanonry. The cathedral was
undefended and its interior was thus vandalised: the cathedral's library was destroyed and
paintings, woodwork, windows, images, altars and hangings were defaced before the Earl
of Huntly, the sheriff of Aberdeen, arrived with forces to put an end to the wanton
damage. It was being claimed by the following century that the choir was also brought to
ruins at this time but this was probably an exaggeration if not wholly untrue. The choir
was probably only partially built and housed no furnishings and trappings. What doubtless
did more to reduce it to the ruin to be seen on Gordon's map was time, indifference and
the use of its stonework for other building purposes.[11]

St Machar's did not, however, totally decline. Soon after 1560, it was decided that it
should replace the Snow Kirk and become the sole parish church of Old Aberdeen,
although financial difficulties precluded much necessary repair work and throughout part
of the sixteenth century the post of minister was combined with that of the Principal of
the College. The cathedral that was once served by nearly seventy clerics was now run by
one part-time minister and a nominal bishop whose main interest lay at St Nicholas
Church, New Aberdeen (Area 7).[12] The seventeenth century, however, saw Protestantism
firmly established and the burgh records reveal an increasing interest not only in church
attendance, but also in repair of the fabric of the church. In 1607, for example, amongst
other improvements, the roof was slated, the first major work since lead from the roof and
the bells in Elphinstone's tower had been removed in 1568.[13]

Further damage to the fabric of the church was, however, effected in the name of
cleansing from idolatry and popery during the Covenanting years of 1639–40; and the
bishop's palace was damaged. In spite of the troubled times, William Strachan, the new
Covenanting minister, undertook some impressive renovations which were completed by
1646. The following years of English rule were to undo much of this good work. A fort
was constructed on Castle Hill, and New Aberdeen and the bishop's palace and remnants
of the choir of St Machar's were the quarry for building material. The full effect of this
vandalism was not to be revealed for some twenty years. In 1687 it became clear that the
central tower of the cathedral was in danger of falling, the removal of the choir on the
east having left it without adequate support. Buttress-building was attempted, but holes
were dug too near the tower walls and on 9 May 1688 it collapsed. Although most of the
stonework fell to the east and the heraldic ceiling remained intact to the west, the two
transepts were destroyed and the east end of the nave was damaged. No attempt was
made to repair the damage. Instead the tower and transepts were abandoned and the
cathedral truncated with a wall blocking the surviving arch at the east end of the nave.[14]
In this foreshortened state the parish church at Old Aberdeen was to survive during the
years of Presbyterianism.

114

the chanonry

At the southern end of the bishop's garden (*see* p 110) stood the chaplains' court which held the chambers of twenty or more chaplains. This was constructed in 1519 by Bishop Dunbar with towers at its four corners, the north-west tower housing a kitchen beside it and a draw-well in the centre of the courtyard.[15] The west wing of this building still stands, although in a much altered state.

Also within the precinct was a small hospital founded in 1531–2 by Dunbar to care for twelve poor men.[16] It stood at the north end of the chanonry with the parson of Tullienessle's manse to the east and that of the rector of Monymusk on the west. The building was 100 ft (30.48 m) long by 32 ft (9.75 m) wide, with a timber steeple and bell, and housed twelve small chambers with chimneys, a kitchen and at the east end an oratory. As late as 1725 it still accommodated eight men.[17]

The final removal of episcopacy, just as at the Reformation in 1560, affected Old Aberdeen both religiously and economically. After 1560 many of the manses which stood in the chanonry fell into lay hands. Wealthy families, including the Marquis of Huntly, whose property stood on the site of the present Chanonry Lodge, were initially drawn by the prestige of the bishop's palace, court and cathedral in spite of its fall from past glory. From 1690 they, too, began to drift away.

notes

1   Cowan, 2–8.
2   Orem, 112.
3   Cant, 3.
4   *Ibid*, 3.
5   *Ibid*, 4.
6   *Ibid*, 6, gives details.
7   Macfarlane, *Cathedral*, 9–10.
8   Cant, 7.
9   McRoberts gives a full account of this heraldic ceiling.
10   The *reredos* of the high altar probably stood on a temporary site—against the east side of the crossing (Cant, 9). There would in this case be a temporary wall dividing off the choir that was under construction.
11   Stevenson, *St Machar's*, 3.
12   *Ibid*, 6–7.
13   *Ibid*, 6–7.
14   *Ibid*, 15–6.
15   Orem, 167, 169, 170.
16   *Abdn Reg*, 401–6.
17   Orem, 167, 169, 170.

area 19

Tillydrone **figure 50**

historic sites and monuments known from documentary and cartographic sources

Tillydrone Port

This port provided access to the chanonry, or cathedral precinct, from the north-west but, to date, no archaeological evidence of this structure has been recovered.

historic standing buildings

Tillydrone Motte

The shape of this grass-covered knoll would suggest that it originated as an artificial earthwork, and tradition accepts it as a fortified 'motte' on which an early timber 'castle' was sited. So far, no documentary evidence has been found to support this hypothesis and no archaeological work has taken place. This site is a scheduled ancient monument.

archaeological potential and future development

Almost nothing is known about the archaeology or archaeological potential of this area. No excavations or watching briefs have been conducted in Area 19; nor have any chance finds been reported. Careful archaeological observation should be maintained of developments in parts of this area. In particular, in line with government guidance on planning and archaeology (**NPPG** 5) and its accompanying advice note (**PAN** 42), there

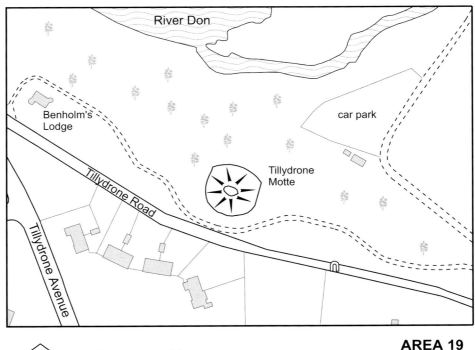

figure 50
Area 19
© Crown Copyright

0   50m

⌂   site of Tillydrone Port

AREA 19

116

Benholm's Lodge (Wallace Tower)

history

This town house was originally constructed in Netherkirkgate, New Aberdeen, in about 1600 (*see* **area 7**). In 1965 it was dismantled to make way for the present Marks and Spencers store, and was re-erected here in Seaton Park.

archaeology

should be a presumption in favour of preservation of the likely motte, and any ground disturbance in its vicinity should be discouraged. No plans for development in this area are currently known.

area 20

Bridge of Don **figure 51**

historic standing buildings and documentary sources

Brig o' Balgownie

Until 1827, this ancient bridge, narrow and steeply pitched above its single pointed arch, was the only route into Aberdeen from the north. Originally dating from the fourteenth century, it was largely re-built at the beginning of the seventeenth century, repaired in the nineteenth century, and the approaches widened and buttressed in 1912. This bridge is a scheduled ancient monument.

archaeological potential and future development

Little is known about the archaeological potential of this area as no formal excavations have taken place, though there is a proven potential at least for post-medieval features (*see Rose Cottage, below*). For the future, any substantial ground disturbance in the area of *Brig o' Balgownie* will require close archaeological observation.

previous archaeological work and chance finds

A *Rose Cottage, Brig o' Balgownie NJ 940 096*

two wells
During work to consolidate a garden wall fronting the former Rose Cottage (demolished in 1968), two wells were discovered behind the wall. The construction date of the cottage

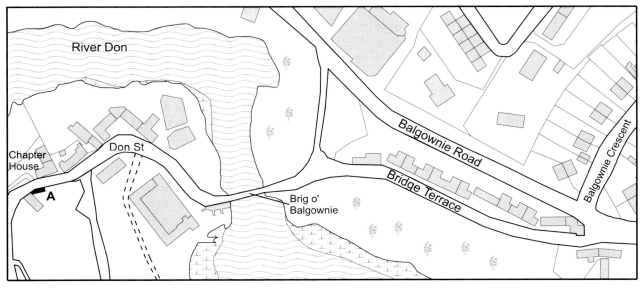

 N   0   50m   ■ archaeological excavation

AREA 20

A   Rose Cottage

figure 51
Area 20
© Crown Copyright

archaeology

and wall is uncertain, but they are first clearly visible on the 1867 Ordnance Survey map. On the wall of one blocked well chamber, 'WI 1856' was roughly incised. There is some evidence that the wells served the so-called 'Chapter House' on the opposite side of Don Street, which may have incorporated a laundry for the Seaton Estate. Both wells were left intact.[1]

note

1   Cameron, *Balgownie*.

Following some twenty years of archaeological excavation, monitoring and developing curatorship within the medieval settlements of Aberdeen and Old Aberdeen, there exist a number of general priorities and directions for future work. More specific objectives are defined within the **area by area assessments**.

1   Publication of the results of all remaining (and future) excavations at both academic and more 'popular' levels. A major publication in the Society of Antiquaries of Scotland monograph series, expected in 1997, will summarise, interpret and discuss in some detail the current state of knowledge of all aspects of the archaeology of the medieval burghs.

2   Focused analysis of local artefactual evidence, such as ceramics, from the medieval and later burghs.

3   Wider dissemination of information about the City's rich archaeological heritage to interested professionals and to the public, through booklets, leaflets, exhibitions, interactive media and educational initiatives.

4   Recognition of the importance of archaeology within any assessment of environment, particularly in the more rural areas on the City fringes, where traces of local prehistory need protection and presentation to the public.

5   Continued rigorous monitoring of potential threats to the archaeology of all periods, both below and above ground, from Mesolithic to World War II and beyond. Arrangements for archaeological intervention where necessary.

6   Further exploitation of documentary sources to inform and illuminate archaeological research and interpretation.

7   Examination of multiple sources to increase understanding of the relationship between burghs and their hinterlands.

gazetteer

pp 120–4

**gazetteer
of significant
sites and finds**
outwith
the historic burghs
of New and Old
Aberdeen

introduction

The sites listed here lie outwith the boundaries of the medieval burghs of Old and New Aberdeen, but within the modern city district. They fall into two categories.

- Known sites of medieval beginnings.

- A range of sites (in many cases industrial) which originated or developed in the eighteenth century.

Actual or approximate locations, where known, can be found on **figures 3, 8 & 42**. The sites are included here to highlight their importance in the continuing process of recovering evidence for the history of Aberdeen, and to ensure that their existence is taken account of in the event of any future development proposals in their vicinities.

There was a vast growth of industry in Aberdeen in the nineteenth century, which falls outwith the remit of this current work. This section contains a summary of the evidence (mainly from cartographic and documentary sources) of a range of industries situated around the burgh, which originated or expanded during the course of the eighteenth century. In some cases these early modern developments themselves destroyed or were built over industrial sites of the medieval period, as perhaps at Justice Mills (Area 14), where eighteenth- to nineteenth-century buildings, demolished as late as the 1930s, may have been constructed on a site used for milling since the fourteenth century. The industrial history of Aberdeen is an area which requires much more research in general; the sites included here are merely those where some background is presently known.

medieval chapels

Stoneywood Chapel
In 1367 the estate of Auchriny was granted by David II to his physician, David Bannerman, with an obligation to complete the chapel, dedicate it to St Mary and instigate a weekly mass for Robert Bruce. In 1649 the chapel is mentioned in the Kirk Session Records of Old Machar.[1] The outline of the chapel is still clearly visible.

St Fergus Chapel, Dyce
This ruined church in a bend of the River Don is a medieval foundation. However, its location and association with two Pictish stones suggest an earlier origin for the site.

Pitfoddels Castle

This medieval motte and bailey castle, located some 6.5 km west of the city centre, controlled a nearby ford across the River Dee.[2] Originally Pitfoddels belonged to the Murray family, passing in the late fourteenth century to the Reids. In the early sixteenth century, Thomas Menzies married Mariote Reid, its heiress. It remained in the hands of the Menzies until 1843. A substantial portion of the motte hill remains, despite damage in recent times. The motte is a scheduled ancient monument.

Freedom Lands boundary markers

In a charter of 1319, Robert the Bruce granted to the burgh of Aberdeen his hunting lands in the Forest of Stocket. These lands were known from then on as the Freedom Lands, and were marked by a series of stones. At first ten large stones, the number was increased in 1578, and again in the period 1790 to 1810, to give the current total of sixty-seven markers. Perambulation of the boundary by the burgh council members is recorded from 1525 to 1889.[3]

coin hoards

As well as the coin hoards found within the burgh boundaries (*see* **Areas 3**, **4**, **7**, **11** *&* **12**), six other coin hoards have been found in the surrounding countryside, as follows.

Baads, Peterculter
An apparently seventeenth-century coin hoard, found about 1852, reportedly contained 'twenty-two foreign coins in silver'.[4]

Binghill, Peterculter
Before 1795, an Aberdeen advocate and farmer, Mr Watson, reported that 'In digging up the foundations of some walls ... my workmen found a handful of silver coins, about the size of sixpences, inscribed *Davidus Rex*', suggesting that this was a medieval hoard.[5] Interestingly, the Latin form of the king's name does not in fact appear on his coins.

Balgownie Crescent, Bridge of Don
A hoard of 197 coins was found in 1937 in a pottery jug, possibly associated with traces of a building and a cobbled floor. A date of *c* 1466 or shortly thereafter has been suggested for its deposition.[6]

Mill of Maidencraig, Lang Stracht In 1858, during excavations on the Skene Road for a new mill dam, workmen found a red earthenware vessel containing 'a considerable number of old coins'. The finders broke the *pint pig* and divided the contents, but the Procurator Fiscal later retrieved sixty-eight English and Scottish coins, ranging in date from *c* 1583 to 1607.[7]

Bankhead Farm, Newhills
In 1862 the farmer at Bankhead farm discovered a 'pose' of silver coins secreted beneath the paving of an old cowhouse. There were thirty-two coins, chiefly of the reigns of Elizabeth I and James VI, but including a Spanish dollar of 1634.[8]

Brimmond Hill, Newhills
A hoard of seventy-seven coins was found beneath a small boulder near the summit of the hill in 1942. The coins appear to have been of sixteenth- and seventeenth-century date, and may have been deposited in the ground during the Covenanting Wars of 1639–46.[9]

Bridge of Dee

Started in the early sixteenth century, by Bishop William Elphinstone, construction of the Bridge of Dee was continued under his successor, Bishop Gavin Dunbar. It was restored in 1720 and, later in the eighteenth century, the chapel at the north end and the port at the south were removed. In the nineteenth century the bridge was widened.[10] It is a scheduled ancient monument.

textile production

Bleachfields are a prominent feature of Taylor's map of 1773.[11] These belonged to the textile companies which operated in the city. Until the latter half of the eighteenth century, textile work had been a cottage industry, with merchants buying in raw materials to be distributed among hundreds of workers, and then collecting the finished product to be bundled together and sold.[12] Litsters and weavers had been of great importance in the trades guilds, since their inception at the beginning of the sixteenth century, but by the end of the eighteenth century, their importance had waned a little—'at one time the weavers were very numerous in the city, and their society was the most influential of all the crafts, but the sound of the hand loom has almost entirely ceased.'[13]

The reason for the decline in hand-weaving was the introduction of steam- or water-powered looms. For example, Alexander Hadden & Sons built a mill in the Green in 1798, using two steam engines. The largest works, however, were established to the north, at Woodside, on the banks of the Don. In 1749 Leys, Masson & Co founded the Grandholm (linen) Mills, on the site of a paper mill which had been founded in 1696, but had failed. To the east of Grandholm were the Gordons mills belonging to Milne, Cruden & Co, who had begun production of linen at the northern end of Gallowgate in 1763. Gordon, Barron & Co, who introduced cotton manufacture to Aberdeen in 1779, also had a mill and bleachfield at Woodside, producing cotton for their workshops in Schoolhill. Wool processing, too, was carried on in this area, Alexander, Hadden & Co having a mill there.[14] Little trace remains of the original buildings, due to subsequent development of the site.

paper mills

As noted above, there had been a paper mill at Woodside in the last decade of the 17th century, but it was defunct by 1749. In 1751, a paper mill, the Waulkmill of Craigton, was founded at Culter, some eight miles west of the city. Stoneywood Mill, just south of Dyce, was founded by Alexander Pirie in 1771.[15]

tile and brick works, and potteries[16]

Also evident on Taylor's map (1773) are the brick kilns and 'brick and Tyle work' at Clayhills. As these areas (Bon Accord Street/Springbank Terrace and Old Ford Road/North Esplanade) are now built-up, there may be little chance of finding physical remains of the structures used in this industry.

On 3rd October 1749 an advertisement appeared in the *Aberdeen Journal*, to announce that John Auldjo, a maker of pan-tile and brick at Clayhills was to begin the manufacture there of brown earthenware. How long Auldjo had been making bricks and tiles is not known—there is some confusion over the date of Paterson's eighteenth-century map of the area. Certainly, there are no brickworks marked on Parson Gordon's map of 1661. By 1799, John's son, George, had run into financial difficulty and had to sell off the whole business.

In Old Aberdeen, at Seaton, there was another brickworks, belonging, in 1778, to Alexander Annand & Company. This works is shown on Taylor's map (1773), and is documented well into the nineteenth century.

The Taylor and Milne maps, of 1773 and 1789 respectively, show a pottery at Footdee (Futty, *see* **area 12**). What is more, between the two dates the pottery appears to have expanded. As with Clayhills, it is not known how long the pottery had been in use, though there is mention of a kiln, used by Robert and Alexander Cruikshank in 1625, in the Aberdeen Shore Works Accounts. Footdee Pottery had ceased production by 1799, as the advertisements for the sale of Clayhills pottery at that time refer to it as 'the only one in this country'.[17]

corn mills

In addition to the medieval mills established within the burgh (the Upper (Area 3), Nether (Area 10), and Mid (Area 7)), and the Justice Mills (Area 14), another mill, at Gilcomston, was erected in 1513. In 1679 the burgh council bought the lands of Gilcomston, including the mill.[18] In 1616, Maidencraig Mill, two Shore Mills, and Bucksburn Mill were built. Milne suggests that this was to have as many mills as possible included in the charter granted to the city by James VI in the following year.[19] At Woodside, there had been a corn mill, Gordon's Mill, at the site which was later used by textile companies (*see above*).

quarries

The burgh council gave permission in 1603 for John Meason to establish a quarry for stone for window-sills and lintels, though precisely where this quarry was situated is not clear. In

1730, however, a quarry was started just to the west of the burgh, in Rosemount, by James Emslie of Loanhead, and in 1741 Aberdeen's most famous quarry, at Rubislaw, was opened. The production of stone from Rubislaw was disturbed by the Jacobite Rising of 1745, and was sporadic afterwards. At a meeting of the council on 7th June 1788, it was suggested 'that the quarry in the Den of Rubislaw should, as the stone is of poor quality and of no use for building, be disposed of to Mr Skene for the sum originally paid for it, namely £160 Scots.' On 26th June, the council agreed to the sale. The Gibbs family took over and, having cleared the poor stone near to the surface, found the high quality granite which was to make the quarry famous in the nineteenth century.[20]

brewing

In 1760, a distillery company bought a lint mill and associated croft at Gilcomston. At first it produced spirits, and then, in 1766, it changed to the brewing of beer.

engineering

Engineering works were established by W McKinnon & Co, at Spring Garden, between George Street and Gallowgate, in 1798; and in Ferryhill by James Abernethy & Co in the same year.

infirmary at Woolmanhill [21]

After the Reformation, the care of the sick ceased to be the responsibility of the Church. By the beginning of the eighteenth century it had become clear that some form of civic provision for the ill, the poor and the insane was needed. In February 1739, the town council of Aberdeen announced that an infirmary was to be founded for this purpose, modelled on the institutions founded in Edinburgh and Glasgow (in 1729 and 1733 respectively). Like the Town's Hospital in Glasgow, the Aberdeen Public House was to be a joint workhouse and infirmary. A site on the north side of Castle Street was proposed, but at a meeting of the directors of the new institution, in November 1739, it was decided that the infirmary would be established at Woolmanhill, and the workhouse at the original site near to the tolbooth. The Woolmanhill site was preferred for the goodness of its air, and the proximity of the Well of Spa, a medicinal spring. On 14th June 1742, the infirmary was officially opened. The building was extended in 1755 and the 1760s, but these buildings were demolished and replaced with the present Archibald Simpson designs in 1840. The Well of Spa, which once stood on the western side of the infirmary, is now situated on the corner of Gilcomston Park Street and Skene Street.

notes

1	Scottish Notes and Queries, 3rd series, vol II, 185–6 (February 1924).	8	*Ibid*, 333.
		9	*Ibid*, 334.
2	Stell, 1972, 180, *no* 18; Stell, 1985, 14, *no* 18; Bogdan, 1988, 16.	10	Brogden, 133–4.
		11	*See* **cartographic sources**.
3	A brochure and map are available from the City Planning and Strategic Development Department, St Nicholas House, Aberdeen.	12	Keith, 307.
		13	Bain, 303–4.
		14	Keith, 307–10.
		15	Milne, 227.
4	Evans and Thain, 333.	16	Evans, G, 8–14, 17–19 & 40–41.
5	*Ibid*, 331.	17	*Aberdeen Journal*, 22 April 1799.
6	*Ibid*, 330.	18	Milne, 226.
7	*Ibid*, 333.	19	*Ibid*, 227.
		20	Diack, 26–29.
		21	Levack and Dudley, 9–30.

alderman	Chief burghal officer, sometimes called praepositus—later provost.
artefact	Object made or built by humans.
assemblage	Collection of artefacts.
backlands	The area to the rear of the burgage plot, behind the dwelling house on the frontage. Originally intended for growing produce and keeping animals; site of wells and midden heaps, *etc*. Eventually housed the working premises of craftsmen and poorer members of burgh society.
back yetts	Small gates in fencing, at end of tofts.
bailie	Burgh officer who performed routine administration often under an alderman or praepositus.
booth	Small open-fronted stalls, sometimes free-standing, but often appended to the front of houses lining the street, where merchants and craftsmen sold their goods.
boundaries	*see* burgage plot
burgage plot	A division of land, often of regular size (having been measured out by liners), allocated to a burgess. Once built on it contained the burgess' house on the frontage (the part nearest the street) (*see* frontage) and a backland (*see* backlands). In time, with pressure for space, the plots were often sub-divided—repletion. Plots were bounded by ditches, wattle fences or stone walls.
burgess	Person who enjoys the privileges and responsibilities of the freedom of the burgh.
burgh fermes	Rentals on property in the town.
common good	Revenues from the burgh courts, the fishings, multures, market tolls, rentals, *etc*.
cordiners	Leather workers.
environmental remains	Denotes a range of non-artefactual evidence from a site, for example animal, fish or bird bones, carbonised wood or grains, seeds, pollen, parasite eggs, *etc*.
feu-ferme	Payment of burgh dues to the crown by pre-agreed annual sum.
fluvioglacial	Deposits of gravel, sand and clay carried by ice-sheets, and deposited by water.
frontage	Front part of burgage plot nearest the street, on which the dwelling was usually built.
gap sites	Burgage plots not built up or 'biggit'.

126

geo	Long, narrow, steep-sided cleft or inlet formed by erosion in coastal cliffs.
hammermen	Metalworkers and associated craftsmen.
heid-dykes	Small, contiguous fencing at tail end of tofts, often containing small back yetts, or gates, giving access to burgh common land and countryside.
hinterland	The rural area around a burgh to which the burgh looked for economic and agricultural support; the hinterland was likewise dependent upon the burgh market.
humic soil	Soil with a high organic content.
indwellers	Unprivileged non-burgess dwellers in a town.
liners	Burgh officers with responsibility to measure burgage plots and supervise building matters.
market repletion	The use of an open market area for building when space became limited.
metasedimentary	Rock composed of layers originally laid down as sediments.
midden	Dump for domestic refuse.
motte and bailey castle	Earthwork castle formed of a large mound encircled by a ditch or ditches, the mound normally topped by a timber wall enclosing a wooden tower. A bailey (outer enclosure) was sometimes provided to give room for ancillary buildings.
multures	Payments for use of town mills.
natural	The level of subsoil undisturbed by human activity.
pend	A covered access between or under buildings.
port	Gate into the town. Shut at night and in times of plague or external danger. Usually a simple wooden structure; occasionally a more elaborate stone feature.
repletion	*see* burgage plot.
rig	Another name for burgage plot.
scarping	Removal of earth, often to provide level ground prior to building.
sill-beam	wooden beam, placed on a bed of stones to form the foundation of a wattle or plank wall.
slag	Waste products from metalworking.
toft	Another name for burgage plot.

tolbooth
The most important secular building; meeting place of burgh council; collection post for market tolls; often housed the town gaol.

tolls
Payment for use of burgh market.

Town House
The principal modern civic building.

tron
Public weigh-beam.

urban nucleus
Original site(s) from which town developed.

wattle
wattle and daub
post and wattle
Principal method of constructing a wooden fence or wall. Pliable branches (wattles) are woven together in between upright posts and, as reinforcement or insulation, daub, layers of clay, mud and animal dung were applied to the wattle surface. Wattle was also used to line pits, wells and drains, and in other constructions such as ovens.

bibliography

pp 128–133

Sources in the keeping of Aberdeen City Archives

New Aberdeen
MS Aberdeen Council Register.
Alphabetical Index to the First Volumes of the Council Register of the City of Aberdeen.
MS Burgh Sasine Register, Aberdeen.
MS Box 33/17.
MS Parcel N.6. Schedule and description of the several properties which will be affected by the proposed south entry into Aberdeen.
MS Press 19, bundle 24.
MS Press 19, bundle 130, Property Register.
Aberdeen University Library, Ms M390.

Old Aberdeen
MS Old Aberdeen Town Council Minutes Books i and ii.
Aberdeen University Library Archives.
MS M390, Mass 8/1.
MS M390, Mass 15/1.
MS M390, Mass 9/1.

printed primary sources

Abdn Chrs Anderson, P J (ed), 1890 *Aberdeen Charters and Other Writs Illustrating the History of the Royal Burgh of Aberdeen* (Aberdeen).
Abdn Eccl Recs Stuart, J (ed), 1846 *Selections from the Ecclesiastical Records of Aberdeen, 1562–1681* (Spalding Club).
Abdn Recs Dickinson, W C (ed), 1957 *Early Records of the Burgh of Aberdeen, 1317, 1398–1407* (Scottish History Society).
Abdn Reg Innes, C (ed), 1845 *Registrum Episcopatus Aberdonensis* (Spalding and Maitland Clubs).
Aberdeen Council Register Stuart, J (ed), 1844–1848 *Extracts from the Council Register of the Burgh of Aberdeen,* (Spalding Club).
Aberdeen Description Gordon, J, 1660 *Abredoniae Utriusque Descriptio* (Spalding Club, 1842), C Innes (ed).
Aberdeen Fasti Innes, C (ed), 1854 *Fasti Aberdonenses: Selections from the Records of the University and King's College of Aberdeen* (Spalding Club).
Aberdeen Friars Anderson, P J (ed), 1909 *Aberdeen Friars Red Black White Grey: Preliminary Calendar of Documents* (Aberdeen).
Aberdeen Journal
Accounts, Extracts *Extracts from the Accounts of the Burgh of Aberdeen,* 1852 Miscellany of the Spalding Club, v, (1852).
Anderson, P J (ed), 1889 *Records of Marischall College and the University* (New Spalding Club).
APS Thomson, T and Innes, C (edd), 1814–75 *The Acts of the Parliaments of Scotland* (Edinburgh).
Bryce W Moir, 1909 *The Scottish Greyfriars* (Edinburgh).
Burgh Records, Extracts (a) *Extracts from the Burgh Records of Aberdeen 1398–1570,* 1844 (Spalding Club).
Burgh Records, Extracts (b) *Extracts From the Burgh Records of Aberdeen. 1643–1747,* 1872 (Burgh Records Society).
Council Register, Extracts *Extracts from the Council Register of the Burgh of Aberdeen, 1625–1642,* 1871 (Scottish Burgh Records Society).
Donaldson, G (ed), 1949 *Accounts of the Collectors of Thirds of Benefices* (Edinburgh).
Douglas, F, 1782 *A General Description of the East Coast of Scotland* (Paisley).

ER Stuart, J *et al* (edd), 1878-1908 *The Exchequer Rolls of Scotland* (Edinburgh).

Gordon, James, 18—, *Aberdeen 1661: Abredoniae novae et veteris descriptio*, Edinburgh, W & A K Johnston.

Innes, Colin, *Plan of the Intended South Entry to Aberdeen, 1798.*

Libellus de Vita et Miraculis Sancti Godrici (Surtees Society, 1847).

New Statistical Account The New Statistical Account of Scotland, vol xii (Edinburgh). The entry for Aberdeen was written in 1845, drawn up by William Henderson, MD, with articles by various other authors.

Old Abdn Recs Munro, A M (ed), 1899 *Old Aberdeen: Records of Old Aberdeen* (Spalding Club).

Old Statistical Account The Statistical Account of Scotland, 1791–99, ed Sir John Sinclair, vol xix (Edinburgh). The entry for Aberdeen was written in 1798, drawn up 'From the Communications of several Gentlemen of that City'.

Orem, W, 1832 *A Description of Old Aberdeen, the Chanonry, Cathedral, and King's College of Old Aberdeen in the years 1724–25* (Aberdeen).

Pennant, T, 1771 *A Tour of Scotland, 1769* (London).

RMS Thomson, J M *et al* (edd), 1882–1914 *Registrum Magni Sigilii Regum Scotorum* (Edinburgh).

Rotuli Scotiae MacPherson, D (ed), 1814-19 *Rotuli Scotiae in Turri Londinensi et in Domo Capitalari Westmonasteriensi Asservati, et al* (London).

RRS Barrow, G *et al* (edd), 1960 *Regesta Regum Scottorum* (Edinburgh).

St Nich Cart Cooper, J (ed), 1888-92 *Cartularium Ecclesie Sancti Nicholai Aberdonensis* (New Spalding Club).

secondary sources

Anderson, J, 1794 *General View of the Agriculture and Rural Economy of the County of Aberdeen* (Edinburgh).

Bain, E, 1887 *Merchant and Craft Guilds: A History of the Aberdeen Incorporated Trades* (Aberdeen).

Bogdan, N Q and Bryce, I B D, 1988 *Directory of the Castles, Manors, and 'Town Houses' of Scotland (c 1052–c 1707)*, Scottish Castle Survey and Architectural Heritage Society of Scotland (NE Group).

Booton, H, 1985 'Economic and social change in later medieval Aberdeen' in Smith (ed), *New Light*, 46–57.

Booton, H, 1988 'Inland trade: a study of Aberdeen in the later Middle Ages' in Lynch *et al* (edd), *The Scottish Medieval Town*, 148–160.

Booton, H, 1990 'Sir John Rutherfurd: A Fifteenth-Century Aberdeen Burgess' *Scottish Economic and Social History*, vol 10, 21–37.

Booton, H, 1993 'The Craftsmen of Aberdeen between 1400 and 1550', *Northern Scotland*, xiii (1993), 1–19.

Brogden, W A, 1986 *Aberdeen, an Illustrated Architectural Guide* (Aberdeen).

Brooks, A J S, 1889–90 'Technical Description of the Regalia of Scotland', *Proc Soc Antiq Scot*, xxiv (1889–90), 49–141.

Brown, J J, 1985 'The social, political and economic influences of the Edinburgh merchant elite, 1600–1638' (unpublished PhD thesis, University of Edinburgh).

Cameron, A S, 1991 'Brig o' Balgownie', *Discovery and Excavation in Scotland*, 1991, 24.

Cameron, A S, 1988 'John Smith's Warehouse, Aberdeen', *Discovery and Excavation in Scotland*, 1988, 13.

Cameron, A S (forthcoming) 'Excavations at Gallowgate Middle School, Aberdeen', *Proc Soc Antiq Scot*.

Cameron, A S, 1992 '16–18 Netherkirkgate, Aberdeen', *Discovery and Excavation in Scotland*, 1992, 35.

Cameron, A S, (forthcoming) 'Excavations at 16–18 Netherkirkgate, Aberdeen', *Proc Scot Antiq Scot*.

Cameron A S, 1993 'St Nicholas Triangle, Aberdeen', *Discovery and Excavation in Scotland*, 1993, 32.

Cameron, A S, Johnston, A and Stones, J A (forthcoming) 'Two Sites in Old Aberdeen', 131
Proc Soc Antiq Scot.

Cameron, A S, and Stones, J A, (forthcoming) 'Excavations at 30–46 and 43–57 Upperkirkgate'.

Cant, R G, 1976 *The Building of St Machar's Cathedral, Aberdeen* (Aberdeen).

Clark, A, 1945 *Aberdeen and the Monks of Aberbrothoc* (Aberdeen).

Cooper, Prof, 1903–4 'The Old Greyfriars Church, Aberdeen: An account of particulars brought to light in the process of its demolition', *Trans Scot Ecclesiol Soc*, 7 part 1, 71–87.

Cowan, I B, 1980 *St Machar's Cathedral in the Early Middle Ages* (Aberdeen).

Cowan, I B, and Easson, D E, 1976 *Medieval Religious Houses: Scotland*, second edition (London).

Cripps, J, 1985 'Establishing the topography of medieval Aberdeen', in Smith (ed), *New Light*, 20–31.

Devine, T M, 1983 'The merchant class of the larger Scottish towns in the seventeenth and early eighteenth centuries' in Gordon and Dicks (edd), *Scottish Urban History*, 92–111.

Diack, W, 1949 *The Rise and Progress of the Granite Industry in Aberdeen* (Aberdeen).

Discovery and Excavation in Scotland, published annually by the Council for Scottish Archaeology (Edinburgh).

Diverres, A H, 1965 'Britain in Froissart's "Meliador"' in Whitehead *et al* (edd) *Medieval Miscellany Presented to Eugene Vinaver*, 97–112.

Duncan, A A M, 1973 *Scotland: The Making of the Kingdom* (Edinburgh).

Evans, D H (forthcoming) 'Excavations at 45–47 Gallowgate'.

Evans, D H and Thain, S, 1989 'New Light on Old Coin Hoards from the Aberdeen Area', *Proc Soc Antiq Scot*, 119 (1989), 327–344.

Evans, G (ed), 1981 *Aberdeen Ceramics* (Aberdeen).

Ewan, E L, 1984 'Burgesses of Fourteenth-Century Scotland' (unpublished PhD thesis, University of Edinburgh).

Ewan, E L, 1985 'The Age of Bon-Accord' in Smith (ed) *New Light*, 32–45.

Fraser, G M, 1986 *Aberdeen Street Names* (Republished with supplement by M Anderson, Aberdeen).

Fraser, G M, 1904 *The Green and Its Story* (Aberdeen).

Fraser, G M, 1905 *Historical Aberdeen* (Aberdeen).

Fraser, G M *Notes and Jottings* in Aberdeen City Library (local collections; index to same).

Fraser, I, 1989 'The Later Medieval Burgh Kirk of St Nicholas, Aberdeen' (unpublished PhD thesis, University of Edinburgh, 1989).

Galbraith, J D, 1982 *St Machar's Cathedral: The Celtic Antecedents* (Aberdeen).

Gibson, A J S and Smout, T C, 1995 *Prices, Food and Wages in Scotland* (Cambridge).

Gordon, G and Dicks, B, 1983 *Scottish Urban History* (Aberdeen).

Graham, C (ed) nd *Aberdeen: Historical Walk-about* (City of Aberdeen Department of Development and Tourism).

Henderson, D, 1982 *The Healers: A History of Medicine in Scotland* (Edinburgh).

Hume, J R, 1977 *The Industrial Archaeology of Scotland, vol II, the Highlands and Islands* (London).

Hunter, J, 1972–4 'The Church of St Nicholas, Aberdeen', *Proc Soc Antiq Scot*, 105 (1972–4), 236–47.

Keith, A, 1972 *A Thousand Years of Aberdeen* (Aberdeen).

Kelly, W, 1933-4 'Carved oak from St Nicholas Church in Aberdeen', *Proc Soc Antiq Scot*, lxciii (1933–4), 355–365.

Kennedy, W, 1818 *Annals of Aberdeen* (London).

Levack, I D and Hugh, D (edd) 1992 *Aberdeen Royal Infirmary: The People's Hospital of the North-East* (London).

Lynch, M, 1988 'Social and Economic Structure of the Larger Towns, 1450–1600', in Lynch *et al* (edd), *The Scottish Medieval Town*, 261–286.

Lynch, M, 1989 'Continuity and change in urban society, 1500–1700', in Houston and Whyte (edd), *Scottish Society, 1500–1800*, 85–117.

132

Lynch, M (ed) 1987 *The Early Modern Town in Scotland* (London).

Lynch, M, Spearman, M and Stell, G (edd), 1988 *The Scottish Medieval Town* (Edinburgh).

McCartney, C, 1979 *The Stained Glass Windows of St Machar's Cathedral, Aberdeen* (Aberdeen).

MacDonald, A A, Lynch, M and Cowan, I B (edd), 1994 *The Renaissance in Scotland* (Leiden).

Macfarlane, L J, 1979 *St Machar's Cathedral in the Late Middle Ages* (Aberdeen).

Macfarlane, L J, 1982 *King's College* (Aberdeen).

Macfarlane, L J, 1985 *William Elphinstone and the Kingdom of Scotland, 1431–1514* (Aberdeen).

Macfarlane, L J, 1987 *St Machar's Cathedral, Aberdeen, and its Medieval Records* (Aberdeen).

MacGibbon, D and Ross, T, 1887–92 *The Castellated and Domestic Architecture of Scotland from the Twelfth to the Eighteenth Century*, 5 vols (Edinburgh).

McNeill, P and Nicholson, R (edd) 1975 *An Historical Atlas of Scotland c 400– c 1600* (St Andrews).

MacNiven, D, 1977 'Merchants and Traders in Early Seventeenth-Century Aberdeen' (unpublished M Litt thesis, University of Aberdeen).

MacNiven, D, 1986 'Merchants and Traders in Early Seventeenth-Century Aberdeen' in D Stevenson (ed), *From Lairds to Louns*, 57–69.

McRoberts, D, 1981 *The Heraldic Ceiling of St Machar's Cathedral, Aberdeen* (Aberdeen).

Mayhew, N J, 1975 'The Aberdeen Upperkirkgate Hoard of 1886', *Brit Numis J*, 45, 33–50.

Mayhew, N J, 1988 'The Aberdeen St Nicholas Street Hoards of 1983 and 1984', *Brit Numis J*, 58, 40–268.

Meldrum, E, 1978 *Aberdeen of Old* (Aberdeen).

Mellor, R E H and Smith, J S 1986 *A Visitor's Guide to Aberdeen* (Aberdeen).

Milne, J, 1911 *Aberdeen: Topographical, Antiquarian and Historical Papers on the City of Aberdeen* (Aberdeen).

Murray, H K, 1984 'Excavations at 45–47 Gallowgate, Aberdeen', *Proc Soc Antiq Scot*, 114 (1984), 303–13.

Murray, J C (ed) 1982 *Excavations in the Medieval Burgh of Aberdeen 1973–81*, Society of Antiquaries of Scotland, monograph series 2 (Edinburgh).

Murray, J C, 1985 'The Archaeological Evidence', in Smith (ed), *New Light*, 10–19.

Robertson, J, 1839 *The Book of Bon Accord* (Aberdeen).

Scottish Notes and Queries, 3rd series, vol II, 185–8 (February 1924).

Short, A, 1982 *Kirkyard of St Machar's Cathedral, Aberdeen* (Aberdeen).

Short, A, 1985 *Old Aberdeen in the Eighteenth Century* (Aberdeen).

Simpson, A T and Stevenson, S, 1980 *Town Houses and Structures in Medieval Scotland* (Glasgow).

Simpson, G G, 1974 *Aberdeen's Hidden History* (Aberdeen).

Simpson, G G, 1980 *Old Aberdeen in the Early Seventeenth Century: A Community Study* (Aberdeen, reprinted).

Skene, B A, 1685 *A Survey of the City of Aberdeen*, reprinted 1867 in *Memorialls for the Government of the Royal-Burghs in Scotland* (Aberdeen).

Smith, A, 1875 *A New History of Aberdeenshire* (Aberdeen).

Smith, J, 1993 *A Visitor's Guide to Marischal College* (Aberdeen).

Smith, J S (ed), 1985 *New Light on Medieval Aberdeen* (Aberdeen).

Smith, J S and Stevenson, D (edd), 1989 *Fermfolk and Fisherfolk* (Aberdeen).

Smout, T C, 1978 'Coping with plague in sixteenth- and seventeenth-century Scotland', *Scotia* ii, no i, 19–33.

Stell, G, 1972 'Provisional List of Mottes in Scotland' in Simpson, G G and Webster, B (edd) 'Charter Evidence and the Distribution of Mottes in Scotland', *Château Gaillard*, v, 175–92.

Stell, G, 1985 'Provisional List of Mottes in Scotland' in Stringer, K J (ed) *Essays on the Nobility of Medieval Scotland*, 13–21.

Stevenson, A, 1988 'Trade with the South, 1070–1513', in Lynch *et al*, *The Scottish Medieval Town*, 180–206.

Stevenson, A W K, 1982 'Trade between Scotland and the Low Countries in the Later 133
Middle Ages' (unpublished PhD thesis, University of Aberdeen).

Stevenson, D, 1981 *St Machar's Cathedral and the Reformation: 1560–1690* (Aberdeen).

Stevenson, D, 1990 *King's College, Aberdeen, 1560–1641: From Protestant Reformation to Covenanting Revolution* (Aberdeen).

Stevenson, D (ed) 1986 *From Lairds to Louns* (Aberdeen).

Stevenson, S and Torrie, E P D, 1990 *Historic Glasgow: The Archaeological Implications of Development*, Scottish Burgh Survey.

Stones, J A, 1982 '12 St Martin's Lane', in Murray (ed), *Excavations in the Medieval Burgh of Aberdeen 1973–81*, 115.

Stones, J A (ed) 1989 *Three Scottish Carmelite Friaries*, Society of Antiquaries of Scotland, monograph series 6 (Edinburgh).

Stones, J A (ed) 1987 *A Tale of Two Burghs: The Archaeology of Old and New Aberdeen* (Aberdeen).

Stones, J A and Cameron, A S (forthcoming) 'Excavations at Virginia Street, Aberdeen'.

Stringer, K J (ed), 1985 *Essays on the Nobility of Medieval Scotland* (Edinburgh).

Torrie, E P D (ed) 1986 *The Gild Court Book of Dunfermline* (Edinburgh).

Torrie, E P D, 1990 'Historical Glasgow' in Stevenson, S and Torrie, E P D *Historic Glasgow: The Archaeological Implications of Development*, Scottish Burgh Survey, 42–57.

Torrie, E P D, 1992 'The early urban site of New Aberdeen: A reappraisal of the evidence', *Northern Scotland*, xii, 1–18.

Tyson, R E, 1985 'The population of Aberdeenshire, 1695–1755: a new approach', *Northern Scotland*, vi no 2 (1985), 113–131.

Tyson, R E, 1986 'Famine in Aberdeenshire, 1695–1699: anatomy of a crisis', in Stevenson (ed) *From Lairds to Louns*, 32–52.

Tyson, R E, 1988 'Household Size and Structure in a Scottish Burgh: Old Aberdeen in 1636', *Local Population Studies*, no 40 (1988), 46–54.

Tyson, R E, 1989 'The rise and fall of manufacturing in rural Aberdeenshire', in Smith and Stevenson (edd), *Fermfolk and Fisherfolk*, 63–82.

White, A, 1985 'The Reformation in Aberdeen' in Smith (ed) *New Light*, 58–66.

White, A, 1987 'The Impact of the Reformation on a Burgh Community: The Case of Aberdeen', in Lynch (ed) *The Early Modern Town in Scotland*, 81–101.

White, A, 1994 'The Regent Morton's Visitation: the Reformation of Aberdeen, 1574', in MacDonald *et al* (edd) *The Renaissance in Scotland*, 246–263.

Whitehead, F, Diverres, A H and Sutcliffe F E (edd) 1965 *Medieval Miscellany presented to Eugene Vinaver* (Manchester).

Wyness, F, 1972 *City by the Grey North Sea* (Aberdeen).

cartographic sources

Cant, R G, 1976 'The Cathedral Kirk and Chanonrie of Aberdeen'.

Downie, J, 1811 'Plan of the City and Harbour of Aberdeen'.

Gordon, J, 1661 'A Description of New and of Old Aberdeen; with the places nearest adjacent'.

Gordon, J, 18–, *Aberdeen 1661: Abredoniae novae et veteris descriptio*, Edinburgh, W & A K Johnston.

Innes, C, 1798 *Plan of the Intended South Entry to Aberdeen*, (Aberdeen City Archives).

Milne, 1789 'Plan of Aberdeen'.

Paterson, G and W, 1746 'A Survey of Old and New Aberdeen'.

Smith, J, 1810 'City of Aberdeen'.

Taylor, G, 1773 'Aberdeen'.

Wood, J, 1809 'Plan of the Cities of Aberdeen'.

Wyness, F, 1972 'The Royal Burgh of Aberdeen based on James Gordon's plan of 1661', reproduced in Wyness, F, *City by the Grey North Sea* (Aberdeen).

Wyness, F, 1972 'Sketch map showing the early site and names associated with the royal burgh of Aberdeen', reproduced in F Wyness *City by the Grey North Sea*, (Aberdeen).

general index

pp 135–147

147